Pierre Elliott Trudeau: Child of Nature
Prime Ministers of Canada
by Paula Johanson

While every precaution has been taken in the preparation of this book, the publisher assumes no responsibility for errors or omissions, or for damages resulting from the use of the information contained herein.

PIERRE ELLIOTT TRUDEAU: CHILD OF NATURE

First edition. January 14, 2021.

Copyright © 2021 Paula Johanson.

ISBN: 978-1989966426

Written by Paula Johanson.

Table of Contents

Pierre Elliott Trudeau: Child of Nature (Prime Ministers of Canada, #1) . 1
INTRODUCTION 3
CHAPTER 1: BIRTH AND YOUTH 7
CHAPTER 2: STARTING OUT 15
CHAPTER 3: FITTING INTO THE PARTY 25
CHAPTER 4: THE OCTOBER CRISIS AND WAR MEASURES ACT 35
CHAPTER 5: A LADIES' MAN, A FAMILY MAN 43
CHAPTER 6: BUILDING PARKS 53
CHAPTER 7: A LONG WALK IN THE SNOW 61
CHAPTER 8: GAINS AND LOSSES FOR AN AGING TRUDEAU 71
GLOSSARY 81
TIMELINE 83
BIBLIOGRAPHY 85

For Kathy

Pierre Elliott Trudeau 1975

INTRODUCTION

THERE'S A RIVER IN Canada's northern territories that to this day has been seen by few people. Trappers and travellers shared legends of a river valley somewhere in the north and west that was warmer in winter than the frozen mountains. The valley of the Nahanni River was eventually mapped and found not to be a tropical Shangri-La but an area of rough beauty and great physical challenges. Among the first of the very few tourists who have ever paddled a canoe on the Nahanni for recreation was Pierre Trudeau. He was proud to pass laws declaring this area and others to be part of the national park system, protecting these natural places from exploitation by mining or logging.

As a member of Canada's Parliament, Trudeau represented one constituency in the House of Commons from when he was first elected in 1965, to 1984 when he retired. That constituency was Mount Royal, in the city of Montreal. This riding has very clear boundaries, and it can be found easily on a map. There were other interests that he represented as well, making a kind of constituency that is less easily mapped as it was scattered across Canada.

Pierre Elliott Trudeau

TRUDEAU TOOK A STRONGER interest than any other Canadian prime minister before or since his time in visiting the natural places of the country. He did more than travel by train and airplane to every province just to walk from office to office for brief meetings and publicity photos — he went out into parks and wilderness places to hike, ski, or paddle canoes. It is a safe bet that in his lifetime he travelled more miles paddling his own canoe than the total travelled by all of the other prime ministers put together.

"Paddling a canoe is a source of enrichment and inner renewal," Trudeau is quoted as saying, on a CBC website describing the top ten nominees for Greatest Canadian.

This site also notes that Trudeau posthumously received the Bill Mason Award for outstanding contributions to canoeing heritage, an award named for his friend and neighbour.

The story of the life of Pierre Elliott Trudeau does more than begin with his birth and end with his death. "My life is one long curve, full of turning points," he wrote in his latter years. As Canada's fifteenth prime minister, what made him different from the others was more than just his interest in the outdoors and in constitutional rights. He was willing to step outside of his own private interests and serve the needs of the many diverse citizens of a nation larger than most empires. Trudeau was connected to ideals and actions outside of his own life events; he was a lifelong practicing Catholic who nonetheless passed laws which removed homosexuality from the Criminal Code, and improved access to legal divorces and abortions.

Born of a family with longstanding roots from the early days of the French colony of Quebec, he increased immigration and the services for new immigrants to Canada, particularly for refugees. As well, he set out in his youth to determine his identity in conscious efforts that bore fruit in his most celebrated achievements as a prime minister, and were echoed in the events of his final years.

Nahanni Gorge

CHAPTER 1: BIRTH AND YOUTH

THE MAN WHO LATER became Canada's fifteenth prime minister was born Joseph Philippe Pierre Yves Elliott Trudeau on October 18, 1919. It was not unusual for a Catholic family to baptize their son with a string of given names including a couple of saints' names as well as his mother's maiden name. He was always Pierre to the family. As a student, young Pierre tried some different choices for signatures and shorter versions of his name before settling on Pierre Elliott Trudeau as the name he would use throughout his life.

The childhood home of Pierre Trudeau was a house on rue Durocher in Outremont, a middle-class suburb on the island of Montreal. The semi-detached row house stood in a neighbourhood of French-speaking and English- speaking families that included Catholics, Protestants, and Jews. The family's three children were Suzette, born in 1918 as the First World War was ending, Pierre, and Charles junior, born in 1922 and known as Tip.

The Trudeau Parents

The family was economically secure before the children were born, as Charles-Emile Trudeau worked as a lawyer. This short but strong and gutsy French-Canadian also owned and managed a chain of thirty service stations. Never a quiet man, Charles-Emile found it easy to laugh, or swear. While the children were growing, he worked hard most days, then would come home for dinner and check the children's homework from school. He enjoyed playing outdoor sports with his children. Years later Pierre would speak of his father and tell of being taught how to paddle a canoe, fire a rifle, and play poker. The Trudeau name in Canada goes back to 1652, with the arrival of carpenter Etienne Trudeau from France.

Charles-Emile Trudeau married Grace Elliott, the daughter of a Scots-Canadian father who was Protestant and a French-Canadian mother who was Catholic. Raised as a Catholic as civil law in Quebec then insisted for children of a Catholic mother, Grace spoke mostly English to her father and French to her mother. With her gentle manner and soft voice, she was a caring and thoughtful mother to her three children. She taught them music, by playing the piano for them and taking them to concerts and the ballet. As they grew older, Grace taught the children to ski. Her love for motorcycle rides came down to her son Pierre, who as a man found great joy when riding motorcycles. Pierre had her blue eyes and something of her quiet nature to start.

The Trudeau Family

Overcoming Shyness

As a small child, Pierre was sensitive and felt he was too timid. He could easily be frightened by loud voices or rough manners. Being shy was not something he wanted for himself. He made serious efforts to become tough-skinned, braver, and confident.

An early effort came when he began first grade at Académie Querbes in their neighbourhood. It upset Pierre that his friend Gerald O'Conner got to be in the second grade only because he was bigger. Pierre complained to his father that it wasn't fair, that he should be in the second grade too. His father refused to speak to the school principal about the matter, telling Pierre it was his own problem, so he should ask the principal himself. The skinny little boy gathered up all his courage and went to meet with the principal. To his surprise, he received permission to enter the second grade. It was an important lesson for young Pierre, not only about self-reliance but about setting goals and speaking out. He began classes in the English-language stream at Querbes, and when he was fluent in English he switched to the classes given in French.

Another step in Pierre's effort to overcome shyness came when his father taught him to box. The boy began to feel confident, even scrappy and willing to show off his ability to stand up for himself. He told his friends he could box, and let fights be set up with other boys.

Eventually Pierre had enough confidence that when one day at lunch, an older student threw a banana in his soup, he simply pulled it out and threw it in the other boy's soup. This was an error, he quickly learned — younger students were not supposed to get even for the pranks of older students.

The older and bigger student angrily demanded Pierre meet him after school to settle matters. It was clear a fistfight was intended. Pierre stood his ground, said nothing, and tried to look resolute. By the end of the day, the older student came round and said he would let him off this time with a warning. It was something Pierre had not expected, but he never forgot that sometimes a fight could be avoided just by acting confident in his own strength.

Young Pierre certainly acted confident at home. Years later, his brother Tip was approached by a journalist who confided that she was a younger sister, and asked what it was like to be the younger brother when growing up in their family. He laughed, and said, "Pierre always had to have the last word."

Good Fortune

While Canada and most of the world were caught in the economic troubles of the Depression years, the Trudeau family had the good fortune to remain not only financially secure, but to become wealthy. In 1931, Charles-Emile Trudeau sold his chain of garages to the Imperial Oil company for $1.4 million — a fortune at the time and the equivalent of about $18 million in 2010.

The Trudeau family moved to a fine home at the base of Mount Royal. Rather than public schools, the Trudeau children now attended private schools in Montreal — Suzette boarded at Sacred Heart Convent and came home for weekends, while Pierre and Tip attended Jean de Brébeuf College as day students. On Monday mornings, Suzette would be driven downtown to Sacred Heart by a man who worked for the Trudeau household, and Pierre and Tip would be dropped off at Brébeuf as it was on the way. There were extra seats in the car, allowing some young neighbour friends to ride to school with them on Mondays. For the rest of the week, the Trudeau brothers walked to school or paid four cents to ride the streetcar.

At Brébeuf the Trudeau sons were taught by Jesuit priests. Learning Greek and Latin were part of the lessons, and Pierre made special efforts to learn everything he could. Mathematics interested him, and the history of Quebec, including stories of the explorers Pierre-Esprit Radisson and his brother-in-law Médart Chouart de Grosseillers, who helped found the Hudson's Bay Company. Pierre got top marks in all his classes, and hung around with a brainy group of boys known as *les snobs*.

One of his friends introduced Pierre to Roger Rolland, a student at another college. Roger and Pierre hit it off, and remained lifelong friends. They would shock teachers and students alike with the prank of going stiff as a board and falling over, only breaking their fall at the last moment. The Club of the Dying made several such sensations at social events.

Besides fine schools, the family's wealth brought other fine experiences to the Trudeau children growing up. There was a Steinway piano for them to practice playing. A gramophone gave them the opportunity to invite friends over on Sundays, and together they would listen to records of classical music.

Even more exciting for the family was a trip to Europe they made in the summer of 1933. Travelling to Italy, France and Germany for two months was a wonderful experience for Pierre. He enjoyed meeting new people and seeing new places. Sometimes his father would send him into a hotel to see if there were any rooms, or challenge him by asking him to go into a bookstore to find a rare book. Even though Pierre spoke no German or Italian, he would rise to the challenge. Usually he was able to report successfully back to his father.

A Bilingual Home

In the Trudeau household, both French and English were spoken, and the children grew up speaking both languages. The parents often spoke English with each other so the father could practice, but he preferred to speak French to the children as he believed this language was more challenging.

With both languages being used around them all the time, it's no surprise the children were bilingual. They could see their Elliott grandfather speak English with their mother, then turn to speak French with their father. Pierre would often speak English with Suzette and French with Tip. He thought everyone could speak English and French, and was surprised to learn most families spoke one language or the other. In Montreal, in Quebec, and in Canada at large, it was more common for English-speaking and French-speaking Canadians to lead separate lives. With his fluency in both languages and roots in both his heritages as a Canadian of French and Scottish descent, Pierre could not honestly identify himself as exclusively one or the other.

Changes in Fortune

In 1935, Charles-Emile Trudeau died suddenly. At the age of fifteen, Pierre was devastated by the loss of his father. He had learned so much from his father about how to ask questions and argue effectively. Now as he was growing up, there would be no father to rebel against or to make proud of him. He would have to set and meet his own challenges.

It was the worst of luck for the family to lose their father, but they were well provided financially. Pierre and his siblings were able to complete school and go on to university studies without having to worry about tuition expenses, or how they would all be housed.

During his schooling, he learned to speak French without the accent of his father and the neighbourhood of his childhood. At Jean de Brébeuf College, he was reading works by French philosophers and novelists while attending weekly lessons in French pronunciation presented by one of the teachers. These elocution lessons were ignored or even scorned by many of the students. A Quebec accent was natural to most Montrealers, many of whom also used the slang-y French dialect known as *Joual*. To Pierre, it seemed more proper to read and speak about the classic French works in an accent more like that used by their authors. As he became a scholar, he learned to speak with the precision and crisp consonants taught by his teachers, who modeled a kind of French more like that spoken in French universities than on the streets of Montreal.

Elitism in Education

Like most of the few young French-Canadians who enjoyed a private education in the 1930s and 1940s, Pierre was taught he was part of an elite who had responsibilities to run the world around them. His teachers did not champion democracy, but raised their students to be pro-fascist. He was taught he should admire European model leaders who were good Catholic dictators like Mussolini, Salazar in Portugal, Franco in Spain, and even Pétain who collaborated with the Nazis in Vichy France.

At this time Pierre followed the ideology of his teachers. He was not yet the rebel he would later become. At *Brébeuf College* he was a model student, who edited the school magazine, and was admired by his fellow students and even some of the staff. He also wrote essays that showed an elitist attitude about governing the mass of people, and a play set in the future staging a revolution against *les Anglais* (English-speaking society in Canada). The play was set in an imaginary 1976 — which turned out to be the actual year René Lévesque would be elected as leader of the Parti Quebecois, on a promise to hold a referendum on whether Quebec should separate from Confederation.

For university, Pierre opted to study law at the University of Montreal, and found a continuity of ideology among his professors. But the fascist leaders he was taught to admire — even during the Second World War and as late as 1944 — included extremists so terrible that at war's end they were shot as war criminals.

River Adventures

With two of his cousins and three friends, a young Pierre Trudeau made an exciting journey in September 1941. Travelling sixteen hundred kilometers by canoe from Montreal to James Bay, the six young men retraced a route taken by the *coureurs de bois* for the Hudsons' Bay Company.

This was no easy summer holiday, but that seems to have been the point of the trip, at least for Trudeau. Perhaps he wanted to challenge himself to follow the route taken by Radisson and de Grosseillers, and was glad to be equal to the task. The trip began right in the heartland of Canada, as they paddled upstream on the Ottawa River, following the provincial border between Quebec and Ontario, to Lake Temiskaming. A paddler does not have to go many miles north of Ottawa, the national capital, to be in another watershed draining north. After crossing Temiskaming, the party canoed down the Harricana River to James Bay. The area is a wilderness crossed by few roads or railroads.

He wrote to a friend afterwards, telling of times that he and his cousin took their canoe through rapids while their companions portaged around those sections of the rivers. When describing the rough portages, food running low, and the dangers of the rapids, he wrote that life was becoming beautiful. They reached James Bay successfully, and paddled along the ocean shore to Moosonee with the weather turning cold. At the end of their canoe trip, the young men sent their canoes home by train and hitchhiked back to Montreal. Their adventure was made much of in the Montreal newspapers.

CHAPTER 2: STARTING OUT

FOR PIERRE TRUDEAU, there was more to a young man's life than education. He had friends, and a Harley Davidson motorcycle for long rides on country roads. His social life kept him busy with many invitations to parties. Never a wallflower, Trudeau's sense of humour and high-energy manner of presenting himself made him noticed wherever he went. At one friend's home, for a formal event, he arrived in swimming trunks and dove into the pool, just to make a sensation. He attended many debutante dances in a large private home that decades later became the Russian Consulate; in the last years of his life, his law firm was located nearby and he could walk home past the Consulate and remember dancing there.

War service

As the Second World War began, joining the army was voluntary. While many Canadians enlisted in the army or navy, or served in the merchant marine, many French-Canadians refused to enlist in the war effort. The call for Canadians to serve overseas was seen by many French- Canadians as a form of British imperialism imposed on them.

Like thousands of Canadian men during the Second World War, Trudeau was conscripted into the Canadian Army as part of the National Resources Mobilization Act. He chose to join the Canadian Officers Training Corps and served with the other conscripts in Canada. In his later memoirs, Trudeau wrote he was willing to fight overseas in the war, but believed that by doing so he would be turning his back on the people of Quebec who he believed had been betrayed by the federal government's conscription under then-prime minister William Lyon Mackenzie King. During a by-election in 1942 for the Outremont riding, Trudeau was part of the campaign for the anti-conscription candidate Jean Drapeau, who later was to become the mayor of Montreal.

Graduate Studies

As a lawyer, Trudeau was called to the bar in the province of Quebec in 1943. Instead of immediately going into practice as a lawyer, he was free to make other choices. He took a break that summer, hitch-hiking across Mexico. When he went to Harvard in 1944 to further his education, Pierre Trudeau was twenty-five, and still true to the elitism learned from his Catholic-French educators. Till recently he had been pro-fascist, and he disliked democracy. At Harvard, he took classes specializing in political science and economics. It was a bit of a surprise for him to find that writing in English continued to be a personal challenge. While fluently bilingual since childhood, he had largely written in French as an adult student. Now at Harvard he was composing essays on which he scored less than perfect marks. For the first time in his scholastic and academic life, he received a B on a paper, and had to do some serious thinking.

Was it simply writing in English that was the problem? Gradually he came to realize that some of his attitudes about the organization of society were changing, becoming less insular and determinist. He was less of the elitist he had been, in a separate society that he had grown up feeling Quebec needed to be; now he was becoming more interested in democracy and collectivism. It was in 1944 Trudeau wrote an essay in French "L'asceticisme en canot" for the Catholic youth movement's *Journal JEC*. Later translated as "Exhaustion and Fulfillment: The Ascetic in a Canoe", the essay has been re-published many times over the subsequent seventy years, both in biographies of Trudeau and in magazines on the outdoors. In this essay he spoke of the wilderness and the pressures of civilization, and of how patriotism could be learned and understood. He was no longer a Quebec separatist, but rather than becoming simply a Canadian federalist he found a different personal motto. On the door to his dorm room at Harvard he pinned a sign reading: "Pierre Trudeau, Citizen of the World."

While at Harvard, the young Trudeau had to adapt to conditions he had never faced before. He lived in student residence, for one thing — modest housing in dorm rooms rather than in a private home or apartment. His experience camping in the wild had not prepared him for this modest kind of urban housing. After becoming accustomed to his dorm room, in future he was able to stay in rough hostels while travelling, sometimes even sharing rooms with strangers.

When his written and oral examinations for a doctorate were complete, Trudeau left Harvard to study in Europe while writing his dissertation. In Paris at the Sorbonne's *L'Ecole des sciences* he worked on two topics concerned with Canada's constitution — a sign that his later focus on bringing Canada's constitution home was not a new interest, but something which was on his mind for decades. Among the books he read which had lasting influence on his ideas was Slavery and Freedom by Nicolas Berdyaev. Trudeau also studied in the London School of Economics. For the topic of his dissertation, Trudeau chose the interplay between Christianity and Marxism. Years of graduate study had exposed him to new ideas about what constituted a Just Society.

Trudeau never finished his dissertation and so his PhD studies were not formally complete. This turn of events is not unusual; it is common enough that in academic circles such scholars are nicknamed 'ABD' or 'all but dissertation.'

Backpack Traveller

After completing courses in London, Trudeau set out with a backpack on a year-long tour of much of the world. The Second World War had recently ended, and travel was just becoming possible in North Africa and the Middle East, but there were few tourists. Sometimes he travelled with a friend or two such as Jacques Hébert, and sometimes alone. He set aside luxuries and travelled instead as working people did, in cargo boats on rivers and seas, in third-class coaches on trains, on buses in China and other countries. He slept in railway stations, youth hostels, and out in the open some nights.

In France he ate in fine restaurants rated with Michelin stars; in China he ate cheap noodles using chopsticks, and was glad for a hot meal. If no dinner was available, between towns, he'd sleep rough. "*Qui dort, dîne*," was the way he saw it, thinking basically "you're not hungry if you sleep."

"What sets a canoeing expedition apart is that it purifies you more rapidly and inescapably than any other travel," he had already written in "Exhaustion and Fulfillment: The Ascetic in a Canoe," his popular essay. "Travel a thousand miles by train and you are a brute; pedal five hundred on a bicycle and you remain basically a bourgeois; paddle a hundred in a canoe and you are already a child of nature." By those standards, he had moved beyond brute and bourgeois and child of nature, and was becoming a citizen of the world. He wanted to know how he would cope in different countries, meeting people who spoke no language he knew. He was looking for adventure.

He found plenty of it. There was fighting in 1948 between Arabs and the new state of Israel, where Trudeau was arrested by Arab soldiers and charged with spying. He could have been executed, but his release didn't make him proceed with more caution. Later he was attacked by three robbers while exploring the ruins of Ur, the birthplace of Abraham. There were times when a Canadian embassy or British Consul would be called to get him out of trouble with local authorities. On at least two occasions he confused thieves by shouting loudly verses of poetry and waving his arms like a madman. He and his friend were scruffy and simply dressed with nothing worth stealing, and he must have looked insane or sick, so he was left alone.

Working in Ottawa and Montreal

On returning to Canada, Trudeau was no vagabond. Even without a completed PhD, in 1949 he was able to find employment in the Privy Council Office in Ottawa. Under the supervision of Gordon Robertson, Trudeau concentrated on the challenges of developing a constitution that would be made in Canada, by Canadians. To him, federalism was pluralist rather than monolithic like the ethnic nationalism he had left behind. He had come to believe that federalism would respect diversity among people and groups, and would support some socialist trends.

After two years he ended his time as a public servant, returning to Montreal to help found and write for the journal *Cité libre* as a co-director. This magazine had unexpected influence among intellectuals and readers in what came to be called Quebec's Quiet Revolution, and its initially small circulation grew over the years. As well, Trudeau participated in left-wing political groups and became an advocate for several unions. He taught basic business skills to union executives, and also helped to negotiate better contracts with their employers. Many times, he spoke to striking workers, on occasion chiding them for not having the guts to take up arms.

At some points Trudeau would speak out against the Catholic Church's controls over what books, plays, or films were available to the public in Quebec; even so, he continued to attend Mass most Sundays. At another time he called the Liberal party a herd of donkeys. Several activist groups had Trudeau on their committees, including a group called the *Rassemblement*, a political group which began meeting in 1956, speaking out in opposition to the federal and provincial governments.

1956 was also the year Trudeau boated along the mighty Mackenzie River in Canada's Northwest Territories. He rode the length of that mile-wide river on the summer supply barge, with lawyer and poet F. R. Scott and a few friends. Frank Scott was not only a lawyer with expertise in constitutional matters, he wrote eloquently about how collective government interests could manage not to infringe on the rights of the individual. Trudeau learned a great deal from him, and shared many of the same beliefs. It was no surprise to Trudeau that Scott could make sense of political ideals being put into practice, and also write clear and heartfelt poetry describing the people and places in his experience. During their time on the Mackenzie, Scott was deeply affected by the trip, and was inspired to write several poems invoking the expedition. The most famous of these poems is *Fort Smith,* in which he described his friend Pierre standing in the river as "A man testing his strength/ Against the strength of his country."

Teaching law was a challenge Trudeau wanted to try, and at that time a completed doctorate was not required of university faculty members. He applied to teach at the University of Montreal, but on at least three occasions the premier of Quebec, Maurice Duplessis, went so far as to block his path to being hired because of what Trudeau had been writing about the government.

As of 1960, Quebec elected a new provincial government, and some of the changes that Trudeau had been advocating began to happen. When the University of Montreal asked if he would teach there, he was able to accept. Between 1961 and 1965, Trudeau was a researcher there and taught in the Law Faculty as an Associate Professor of Law.

Private Practice

Because he could live on the carefully-invested inheritance from his father, Trudeau never had to work hard just to afford living expenses. That didn't mean he let himself be idle. He wrote, and practiced law, and participated in political groups. As a lawyer working in private practice on rue Saint-Denis in Montreal during the 1950s, he was able to represent cases that interested him without always charging for his services.

Between 1962 and 1965, Trudeau taught two courses for the University of Montreal, on "Constitutional Law and Administrative Law" and "Civil Liberties." In retrospect, some of his students later commented that what Trudeau implemented in 1982 as prime minister was the same approach he talked about in his lectures at the University of Montreal.

While he was teaching at the University, Trudeau took a month's leave of absence without pay to defend writer Jacques Hébert. The controversial publisher had released a book claiming that a miscarriage of justice had occurred during a murder trial. Hébert's case came to court in Quebec City, but Trudeau travelled there and defended him without charging for his services. As well, other friends of Trudeau have acknowledged that he helped them and others professionally and financially, with discretion and privacy.

A Daring Traveller

Sometimes it seemed to his associates in activist groups that whenever a controversy arose in the group, Trudeau would head away to backpack across Asia or the like. He did travel a great deal, more than his friends and associates like Roger Rolland, Marc Lalonde, or Jacques Hébert were able to afford. Many of his travels did coincide with disagreements or controversies among his activist associates, but Trudeau did not seem to be running away from problems so much as avoiding taking sides or adjudicating disputes. From his activities in political and activist groups and writing for magazines, Trudeau was learning how committees function, how plans are made and come to pass, and how to work with associates of varying abilities and different beliefs.

While travelling with a backpack and a friend, Trudeau often ended up sleeping on benches in railway stations or churches. Even on the road, he rarely missed Sunday Mass. When hitch-hiking through North Africa or across Asia, he looked for churches. Even when he couldn't speak the local language, if he could find a Catholic priest he could speak to him in Latin. Being taught by Jesuits paid off many times, helping him to learn where visitors could find a cheap meal and a roof to sleep under.

During his travels, Trudeau found challenges to test himself. While in Turkey during 1948, he looked across the Bosporus Strait and decided to swim it. When Lysander had swum the Hellespont, according to classic Greek verse it was the act of a hero; two thousand years later, the poet Lord Byron swam the strait in his own search for heroic strength. Trudeau swam the strait without any commemorative verses being written, saying much later "It wasn't that hard, but it was cold and had a bloody strong current."

He didn't seem to grow out of this need to challenge himself. At the age of forty-one, he set out with two friends to paddle a canoe from Miami to Cuba. They had gone about half the distance when they were rescued as their canoe began to sink. It's not an easy crossing, and in years to come many people would drown trying to take small boats from Cuba to Florida. The next year, 1961, he was in Pamplona, Spain, partying until three o'clock in the morning. With no hotel rooms available, he fell asleep on a park bench for a few hours and then joined the Running of the Bulls down narrow streets. The experience was so exciting, he did it again two days later.

Writing of Sovereignty

It was in an article for the April 1962 issue of *Cité libre* that Trudeau wrote of the state being a larger entity which could include nations within it, as in the newly- independent Algeria or in India with its four official languages. To him, sovereignty for nations within a state would come at the expense of smaller groups. "The very idea of the nation-state is absurd," he wrote. "To insist that a particular nationality must have complete sovereign power is to pursue a self-destructive end. Because every national minority will find, at the very moment of liberation, a new minority within its bosom which in turn must be allowed the right to demand its freedom." Nation-states, he added, are ways for strong nations to justify their oppression of the weak, leading to dominating errors such as exploitation and colonialist oppression. He argued instead in favour of a constitutional approach to recognize poly-ethnic pluralism within multinational states.

What worried him in particular was that if five million French-Canadians couldn't manage to share national sovereignty with seven million Canadians of British origin, he had little hope that several thousand million Americans, Russians, and Chinese who had never met would ever agree to give up their piece of sovereignty in nuclear arms. How could the world avoid a nuclear war? He was not alone in this worry, and it was not an empty fear, as the Cuban missile crisis demonstrated.

In some ways, this article and others he wrote during these years showed the beginnings of Trudeau as a politician. In 1958, Trudeau wrote an article for Vrai Magazine in which he said: "The true statesman is not one who gives orders to his fellow citizens so much as he is one who devotes himself to their service." He was trying to become a man who could be a true statesman, not a fascist controlling his nation but something closer to a citizen of the world, who could serve his people within a larger state rather than dominate them.

CHAPTER 3: FITTING INTO THE PARTY

AS TRUDEAU BEGAN to take an interest in running for office, he explored some of the alternatives available. Federal politics were what interested him most, more than provincial politics within Quebec or the roles available in local government in Montreal. The goals of the New Democratic Party were similar to his own. The NDP was a new national party of social democrats which had its origins in Canada's western provinces as the CCF or Canadian Commonwealth Federation, a socialist party. But after some time exploring a possible future with the NDP he felt that party's organization didn't satisfy him.

Instead, Trudeau kept up with his writing and looked for other opportunities. *Be ready when opportunity comes*, was later to become a saying of his. *Luck is the time when preparation and opportunity meet.*

For English-speaking Canadians, Trudeau's entry into politics seemed rather abrupt. It was as if he appeared out of nowhere. But then, it wasn't usual for Anglos to be as aware of how their lives were affected by French-Canadian politics as *les Canadiens* and particularly *les Quebecois* were aware of *les Anglais*. Quebec's Quiet Revolution was a series of changes in political beliefs and actions for both French and English-speaking people in Quebec during the 1960s, and it was having effects that spread out into the rest of Canada.

When the federal Liberal party of Canada realized that it was time to take on new members who were French-Canadian, they approached Jean Marchand and asked him to run for office to be a member of Parliament. He insisted the party should also ask his long-time associates, Gerard Pelletier and Pierre Trudeau. With that, these friends known as *les trois coulombs* (three doves), or the Three Wise Men as they were nicknamed in English, entered federal politics as members of the Liberal party.

When Allan Macnaughton, the long-time member of Parliament for the riding of Mount Royal, announced his retirement Trudeau was asked to be the Liberal party's candidate in that riding. He won his seat in the 1965 election, and stayed with this riding throughout his political career. *Reason before passion* became his motto, especially while in politics.

As a first term backbencher in Lester Pearson's Liberal government, Trudeau began to make an impression in caucus. From his first days in Parliament, working for a national constitution was one of his goals. "I believe a constitution can permit the co-existence of several cultures and ethnic groups with a single state," he said in a public statement in 1965. When Pearson offered him a position as provincial secretary to the prime minister, he didn't want it at first, but accepted on advice from Marchand and Pelletier. In eighteen months he was given the cabinet post of justice minister, and he began to take action.

Trudeau, Turner, Chretien and Pearson Change of Cabinet

Sweeping Reforms

PIERRE ELLIOTT TRUDEAU: CHILD OF NATURE

IN 1967, CANADA'S CENTENNIAL year, Trudeau was called to the bar in the province of Ontario. That year and the next, he was the Minister of Justice. Within a year, the divorce laws had been reformed, improving women's access to divorce. New laws were passed, removing consensual homosexuality from the Criminal Code. Trudeau was widely quoted as saying: "The state has no place in the bedrooms of the nation." As well, the laws controlling abortion were changed so that abortion was no longer illegal, but still carefully regulated.

Trudeau had made no secret of his Catholic background, or that he continued to attend Mass most Sundays. The Roman Catholic church did not allow divorce; as well, to the church, any homosexual acts and abortion for any reason were considered great sins. It was rare in Canada — and particularly in Quebec — for an official who was Catholic to speak out in favour of proposed government legislation that disagreed with pronouncements from the Church, even on simpler matters like the rating of films shown in theaters Based on his writings before this time and later in his memoirs, Trudeau wasn't contradicting the church so much as recognizing that these issues were matters of personal conscience, not crimes under criminal law.

It didn't take much for Trudeau as Justice Minister to upset people's expectations. All he had to do was show up for work some days wearing a polka-dotted ascot instead of a discreetly-striped necktie, and many of his colleagues were shocked. Others took more offense when he wore a brown corduroy suit instead of a more sombre dark blue serge, or sandals instead of shoes. When he took to wearing a fresh flower in his lapel, some commentators considered it flamboyant or showy. Among the staid members of Parliament and civil service employees on Parliament Hill, that's all it takes to be flamboyant. Undeterred, Trudeau began a life-long habit of wearing a fresh flower, usually a rose, every working day.

A Leadership Role

On the resignation of Lester Pearson from the post of prime minister in 1968, Trudeau was asked by the party to become a candidate. He won the Liberal leadership convention, and was delighted by this sign of party support. A photographer at the convention caught a candid photo of Trudeau sliding on a banister, and the image appeared in newspapers across the country. Immediately he called an election.

Trudeau moved into the prime minister's residence at 24 Sussex Drive, bringing with him only two bags and his treasured Mercedes 300 SL convertible. He had no real home of his own to leave, having lived in a few apartments and remaining close to his mother as her health deteriorated.

On the day before the June 1968 federal election, Trudeau as leader of the Liberal party was one of several guests invited to attend the parade through downtown Montreal on Saint-Jean-Baptiste day. Sharing the stands with Quebec's Premier Johnson and Mayor Duplessis and other officials, Trudeau was watching the parade pass when a demonstration started right in front of the stands. Separatist members of the *Rassemblement* shouted ugly statements about Trudeau being a traitor for sitting with an Anglo premier and with Duplessis, against whom he and they had campaigned a few years earlier. They caused a scene. Police attempted to keep people back as rocks and bottles were thrown. The mayor and premier retreated, but Trudeau resisted his RCMP escort's advice to leave. He returned to his seat and brazened out the catcalls and bottles, watching the remaining part of the parade, refusing to be driven away by misbehaving demonstrators.

The next day, the election results were decisive. The Liberals won a majority of seats, not only in Quebec but much of Canada. It was a landslide victory that gave Trudeau and the Liberals confidence to pass laws that would lead to sweeping social changes. It's worth noting that the first Royal Assent that Trudeau signed as prime minister, with Governor-General Roland Michener standing in for the Queen as usual, was for the Medical Care Act, which completed Canada's national medicare system. The push to establish medicare began in the NDP from its earliest days as the CCF; it was taken up by the Liberals under Pearson, and the Medical Care Act passed with support from many members of the Progressive Conservatives as well.

Trudeau-mania

The media called the popularity of the prime minister and his party Trudeau-mania, because the swell of public opinion capitalized on his extraordinary public appeal. It's important to remember that prime ministers at that time were not autocrats who ruled alone, but leaders of a cabinet of active and influential ministers. While Trudeau was a front man and a figurehead, he was part of a cabinet and a party caucus that discussed and argued and compromised their way to a plan for action, if not complete consensus. Many of Trudeau's cabinet members were men he knew well like Marc Lalonde, who played an important role in Trudeau's government after working alongside Trudeau in the 1960s in Quebec. Jean Chretien was another cabinet minister, someone whom Trudeau had come to respect as a man who would roll up his sleeves and get work done.

From 1968 to 1984, Trudeau was the party leader of the Liberal Party of Canada, and the prime minister except for a nine-month period in 1979-80 when he was the leader of the opposition. While in office, Trudeau would begin his days with detailed briefings on the meetings he would have that day, confirming information about the people he would see and the issues that were at hand. In strong contrast to the lasting media impression of Trudeau as a leader who made pronouncements without consultation, the prime minister was in fact a leader who co-operated with his cabinet and advisers, consulting many opinions before coming to conclusions and making announcements.

Some commentators spoke of Trudeau as arrogant, but perhaps he gave that impression because he was active and confident, with an excellent memory. Certainly it was not his habit to interrupt members of Parliament speaking in the House, or journalists during an interview; he would wait until the speaker paused for breath and then deliver a quick and often stinging response. Nor did he impose his uninformed opinions as policy. There are stories of meetings where provincial premiers and Trudeau would discuss constitutional issues, and Trudeau's comments could get sharp and barbed when addressing premiers of Quebec. It took René Lévesque responding in kind, and some rapid-fire insults passing back and forth first in French and then in English to allow their colleagues to understand these verbal sallies, for some of the western premiers to understand their dynamic. As Allan Blakeney learned when he was premier of Saskatchewan, "leaders from Quebec — when addressing each other — are often long on invective and short on civility."

Trudeau-mania was a phenomenon outside of Canada as well. Though few Americans took note that Canada had a new prime minister, or a prime minister at all, many Europeans were interested in this new leader. When Canadian musician Oscar Peterson did an extensive tour of Europe, he lost count of how many people in various countries were curious to learn if he knew Trudeau personally. He was impressed by how many Europeans he met who were admirers of Trudeau. Peterson had spoken with the prime minister on many occasions, including a reception where a presentation was made to young classical musicians. In a quiet conversation, Trudeau joked with Peterson about coming back from an official trip abroad just to hear if Peterson could still play piano; then he spotted one of the award winners, who was young and female and pretty.

Quickly Trudeau excused himself, saying that he had to take up part of his duty as prime minister — the proper congratulation of this fine young award winner.

Officially Bilingual Government

One of the most important bills passed during Trudeau's first twelve months as prime minister was the Official Languages Act of 1969. The business of Parliament was already being conducted in both official languages. One of Trudeau's speechwriters, his longtime friend Roger Rolland, wrote his speeches in French. This act guaranteed that the federal civil service would be bilingual, and that services would be available to Canadians across the country in both English and French. There were people who couldn't see any need for some adult civil servants to learn French even in predominantly English-speaking areas, but for many Canadians the idea of bilingual government services promoted a sense of national unity.

An immediate effect of the Official Languages Act was the increased job opportunities for Francophone Canadians who wanted to enter the federal civil service. A close second was the increase in adult education for Anglophones who wanted to learn French. Adult education became a more common practice in language and other areas, not only for those seeking employment but for improvement and promotions.

White Paper

Soon after the Official Language Act, Trudeau's cabinet released an even more controversial statement of proposed policy in a White Paper on Indian Affairs. The status of Aboriginal or First Nations people within Canada definitely needed attention on a federal level. But the proposed policies were met with alarm on Indian Reserves across the country. Among other things, the paper suggested that official Indian status should be eliminated, and that there should be private ownership of land within reserves.

First Nations representatives met in several groups to create various responses to the White Paper, which they considered an effort to abolish treaty rights and to eliminate aboriginals through assimilation. It had not escaped notice that there were absolutely no persons of First Nations descent in Trudeau's cabinet. Even the name "White Paper" was commented upon as an emblem of European-centric attitudes in the Canadian government, when it was in fact a nickname for the finished draft of proposed policy ready for public reading, which would be printed on white sheets instead of yellow draft paper. The First Nations responses included a 'Red Paper' of their own suggested actions, as well as calls for attention to the problems of the residential school system. Among the issues raised was the controversial policy of adoption of First Nations children to Canadians of European descent. From the 1960s until the 1980s, thousands of Metis and First Nations children were taken by child welfare services and adopted into non- aboriginal families, some in the USA, even when the children had relatives able to take them in. In the face of these negative responses, Trudeau and his cabinet backed down and moderated their stance. It seems that Trudeau's personal goals for the status of First Nations people were not for them to disappear but for their status as welcome citizens of Canada to be supported. While in office, he was never able to resolve aboriginal issues to the satisfaction of all concerned. For a politician involved in Quebec's Quiet Revolution and later in Quebec's sovereignty issues, he was surprisingly unable to articulate his own federalism in ways that met

First Nations needs. Perhaps he hoped that for individual aboriginal Canadians their own experiences would be as positive as those in his family and his mother's family, where Canadians of Scots and French descent spoke two mother tongues with confidence. It's worth noting that Trudeau and his wife adopted their youngest son, Michel, who was of First Nations descent.

There was no quick solution. Many of the issues raised in the White Paper and the Red Paper remain unresolved in 2015. Almost 1,200 aboriginal adults who had been adopted filed a class-action lawsuit against the federal government, seeking damages for the sexual and physical abuse some of the adoptees suffered, as well as the loss of cultural identity.

Living Well

As well as the large residence at 24 Sussex Drive, the government of Canada owns a smaller residence for the prime minister's use in Gatineau Park close to Ottawa, a fine home known as Harrington Lake. It quickly became a favourite place for Trudeau, and later for his wife and their sons. They would often spend weekends there, with Trudeau working as necessary and taking time with the family. Boxes of materials he had to study would be couriered there by RCMP officers. Committees of MPs and officials would meet with Trudeau in the house or on the grounds, as a break from meeting on Parliament Hill. During and after elections, workers from the Liberal party would meet there to debrief, then unwind while hiking on the trails or canoeing on the lake.

It's easy to think of a millionaire prime minister as a money man, but Trudeau was not someone who threw his money around. With careful investing and economizing, the inheritance from his father had grown, but he didn't spend his income casually. He came from a generation which believed socks should be mended and people should take care of their possessions. Housekeeping staff at 24 Sussex Drive noticed that the prime minister's favourite hiking boots had belonged to his father, and he cleaned and polished these boots himself. The staff were also aware that he knew the names of housekeepers and groundskeepers, and took an interest in their work and lives. Whenever an official dinner was held at either residence, Trudeau would always step into the kitchen afterwards to thank the staff for their extra work and the fine meal.

Working Lunch at 24 Sussex Dr

His friends insist that he was never heard to boast about his family's wealth or his privileged life. Perhaps he picked up more than his share of restaurant checks, but he was notorious for leaving small tips. While Trudeau did wear a gold Rolex wristwatch, it was regularly serviced and repaired so that it lasted for decades. He strove to treat money with detachment, and to enjoy some pleasures such as travel or his Mercedes convertible car, but without becoming dependent on material goods. This well-maintained Mercedes was already a vintage automobile in 1979. It was eventually inherited by Trudeau's eldest son Justin, who continued to drive it on occasion and in particular on his own wedding day.

CHAPTER 4:
THE OCTOBER CRISIS
AND WAR MEASURES
ACT

CANADA HAS NEVER BEEN a seamless nation of people who all think alike. Since the battle of the Plains of Abraham and the conquering of French colonies by the British, there have been some citizens who called for separation of French-speaking Canadiens from being governed by English-speakers in Canada. By the 1960s the idea of separating Quebec from the rest of Canada didn't seem likely to Anglos, but it was still advocated among some political and social activists in Quebec. The Quiet Revolution seemed to be having results, with a new party in power in Quebec and Trudeau as Canada's prime minister. But there were still those who called for the independence of Quebec.

The FLQ

Some activists were frustrated by a lack of results from their advocacy, and formed a group of extremists calling themselves *Front du liberation de Quebec* (FLQ) or the Quebec Liberation Front. Their statements about Quebec separation were too extreme for most magazines to print, and not popular enough to appear as articles in mainstream newspapers. Publishing their own mass-market magazines and books was not an affordable option for a small group of radicals in the late 1960s; even Trudeau and his co-publishers had found their more politically-moderate magazine *Cité libre* took years before its circulation increased to the point that income covered all the costs. Cheap photocopiers and mimeographs were not generally available even at schools and churches. Self-publishing at that time was done only by a very few poets or fans of music and science fiction, using Gestetners and hectographs only on the scale of a few dozens of copies. Extremist political statements had limited sales appeal for readers.

Some members of the FLQ turned to setting off bombs in mailboxes to arouse public interest in what they had to say. In these bombing incidents, some of which resulted in arrests, there were surprisingly few injuries. While the bombings and resulting court cases were reported, the FLQ statements were not quoted in the media. Since mailbox bombings didn't bring the FLQ enough attention in the media, the extremists among the FLQ resolved to escalate their actions. Canadians in Quebec and elsewhere were nervous about the FLQ, but had little information to go on.

Matters came to a crisis the morning of October 5, 1970, when the British Trade Commissioner, James Cross, was kidnapped from his Montreal home by members of the FLQ. This small cell of people was willing to use violence for their goals. They refused to release Cross unless the federal government agreed to meet their demands. Among these demands were the publishing and broadcasting of their political statements supporting separatism, the release of some of their members who were in prison for criminal acts, and $500,000 in gold.

Trudeau and his cabinet met and did not agree to any of these demands. No one had any idea what would happen, and everyone had opinions about what should or should not be done. While the FLQ claimed to have a hundred thousand supporters, there was no way to verify how few or many people were actually members.

Another group of FLQ members kidnapped the deputy premier of Quebec, Pierre Laporte, on October 10. The crisis was clearly escalating. There were fears that riots would happen — not just a few dozen people hurling bottles and insults, but hundreds of people or more who might destroy property and lives. The mailbox bombings were not forgotten, and what would be the bomb targets now?

Soldiers from the Canadian army were moved into position in Ottawa to protect sites and people connected with the government. As Trudeau entered Parliament on October 13, he paused on the stairs to speak with reporters.

"Society must take every means at its disposal to defend itself against the emergence of a parallel power which defies the elected power," he said to reporters in an interview broadcast that evening on CBC Television with the sound of the clock in the Peace Tower ringing behind his voice. How far would he go to defend the country? asked a journalist, and Trudeau replied plainly, "Just watch me." It wasn't a challenge, it was a reminder that he wasn't acting in secret, and that his actions were subject to public scrutiny.

Trudeau consulted with Jean Drapeau, the mayor of Montreal, and with Premier Robert Bourassa, for their insight on what was happening. At Bourassa's request, the army was called in to help maintain order in parts of Montreal and Quebec City. Trudeau had not forgotten that earlier in the year, Bourassa did not come through on his agreement to support a constitutional agreement among the provinces; for Trudeau, Bourassa's request had to be put in writing so that the Quebec premier could not complain later about the army being deployed.

This movement of troops was not welcomed by all Canadians. Many voices were raised in Parliament and in newspapers, as some people accused Trudeau of taking advantage of the crisis to crush separatism in Quebec. Others, mostly living outside Quebec, praised the decision.

The War Measures Act

As tension mounted, Jean Chretien and other members of the cabinet called for the War Measures Act to be declared. Trudeau agreed that it was necessary. The Act was passed in the House of Parliament, over Opposition protests, early in the morning of October 16. While the War Measures Act was in effect, the civil rights of citizens were suspended to allow special powers for the army, the RCMP and provincial police, and local police forces.

Increased security was necessary for Trudeau, but it was not easy to manage. During the crisis he took a short break over the Thanksgiving weekend. With his fiancée Margaret Sinclair, Trudeau went to the Harrington Lake property so they could be together in privacy. For the lovers, there was no secrecy from the heavy security surrounding the prime minister during the October crisis. One rainy day the pair hiked into the forest and got lost — at least, their RCMP security officers believed they were lost and panicked. As the couple came from the heavy forest into a clearing, they heard gunshots. An officer was in the middle of the lake with an umbrella against the rain, firing a rifle into the air so the sound could guide them home.

It was good that Trudeau was not out of touch when at Harrington Lake, for word came that the body of Pierre Laporte had just been found. It was later learned that on the day the War Measures Act was declared, Laporte had struggled desperately to free himself from captivity, and been injured falling from a window. His captors murdered him and put his body in a car trunk where it was found the next day, October 17.

On the day when Laporte's murder was reported, the experience of learning the news together brought Trudeau and Margaret closer. It was heartbreaking to think of the murder, and of Cross still being held captive.

As they discussed the crisis, Margaret came to understand that her fiancé was more than Pierre, the man she was going to marry. Here was a prime minister making hard decisions. He was resolved not to give in to demands by the FLQ, not even to save lives of hostages. Margaret was appalled to learn that he intended this resolution would include even her or any children they might have, if they were ever kidnapped.

Tensions remained high in Quebec and across Canada as the October Crisis remained unresolved into early winter. The police and armed forces were uncertain whether there would be further hostage events or an escalation of violence. The public and press were uncertain just how many members of the FLQ there could possibly be in Quebec or other parts of Canada. In Montreal and Quebec City, there were English-speaking families who found the crisis spurred their decisions to move their homes and businesses to Ontario or western Canada. The unfamiliar sight of armed soldiers standing guard in major cities was upsetting for Canadians, particularly for those who had survived war experiences. There were few public demonstrations on other issues, as this particular crisis dominated national attention.

Margret Sinclair and Pierre Trudeau

On December 6, the day James Cross was released by his captors, newspapers across the country carried the headline "CROSS FREE!" in letters larger than those used to announce the first Moon landing eighteen months earlier. There was considerably less fanfare when some members of the FLQ were permitted to leave the country on December 26, while other members were arrested. Some of the FLQ's separatist rhetoric was published in newspapers, in part to reduce any sense of mystery or suppression about its contents, which for the most part were rather shrill and dull.

Arrests and Searches

Governments have the responsibility to protect citizens from harm. Usually this protection is thought of as safeguarding national territory from invading armies of outsiders. But how is a government to protect citizens from attacks within the country's borders? The War Measures Act was legislation passed to allow extraordinary powers for law enforcement during a time of crisis. The only time a challenge like this has been faced in Canada was during the October Crisis of 1970.

The effect of the act could be seen almost immediately. People could be arrested and held in jail without being charged with a crime. Within 48 hours of the act being passed by Trudeau's government, almost 250 people were arrested and jailed in Montreal and other Quebec cities. Under the War Measures Act, police could search people or private homes and businesses without needing a warrant. There were 31,700 of these searches done in the next couple of months as police looked carefully for any signs of people involved with the FLQ.

Though almost 500 people had been arrested by year's end, only 62 people were ever formally charged. Some of the people held without charge were arrested in Canada's prairie provinces and the Maritimes, with no apparent connections to the FLQ or to Quebec separatism.

Many people, including members of Parliament and provincial legislatures, were outraged at the loss of rights and freedoms for citizens. Tommy Douglas, the leader of the New Democratic Party, stood up in the House and claimed that the prime minister had used a sledgehammer to crack a peanut. But Trudeau replied that peanuts don't make bombs, don't take hostages, and don't assassinate prisoners. The War Measures Act was not revoked for several months. In its wake, and since the Canadian Constitution was signed, other legislation has been passed which provides some of the protection intended by the War Measures Act but without the sweeping loss of civil rights for all. Decades later under a Conservative government and Prime Minister Harper, anti-terrorism legislation was passed giving extraordinary powers to the Canadian Security Intelligence Service, and the possibility of revoking citizenship for Canadians charged with terrorism.

PIERRE ELLIOTT TRUDEAU: CHILD OF NATURE

Funeral of Pierre LaPort

CHAPTER 5: A LADIES' MAN, A FAMILY MAN

BEFORE HIS MARRIAGE, Trudeau was known to date many women who were educated, or politically active, or in the public eye as actresses and singers. Some of these women remained his friends years later, and spoke of his personal charm and the magnetic appeal he held. It wasn't until he was fifty years old that he seriously considered marriage.

Looking back on his photographs, it's hard for readers in the twenty-first century who see movie-star good looks everywhere in the media, to think of Trudeau as powerfully attractive. The man was known to wear beige corduroy suits, after all. How could a man with big teeth and a narrow chin, with thinning hair meticulously combed over his head, of no more than average height and turning fifty ever be described as having sex appeal? But he was, many times, not only by women he dated but by political journalists who were men.

Videos of Trudeau in interviews give a fairer idea than photographs do of the impression that he could make in conversation; he was alert, attentive and responsive. When he spoke it was with evident intelligence, confidence, and a direct manner. He also had an athletic body shaped by regular exercise. When he moved he looked competent and effective, and was free from the stumbles that afflicted other political figures such as Joe Clark or Gerald Ford.

His charisma was more than a momentary charm between friends. Strangers walking past him on city streets would sometimes turn and stare, even sophisticated career women who didn't recognize him by name at first or second glance. He could have similar effects on groups and crowded rooms.

When Canadian novelist Matt Hughes was a political speechwriter on Parliament Hill, he liked to observe how people reacted to those who were powerful and charismatic. "At a reception, I would stand on the sidelines and try to map the eddies and currents that moved people toward Pierre Trudeau for their brief moments of contact then away into the outer darkness," he noted. "Or the way the waiting crowd would suddenly become more alert the moment he walked into the room."

Not everyone was under his spell. Academic Heidi Tiedemann Darroch wrote of her memory of a school visit to Parliament in her youth. "I remember the day that PET came to Parliament Hill for the unveiling of his portrait, and the horror of standing next to him and feeling awkwardly too tall." She added, "Hope his statue's more-than-life-sized."

His Bride

Trudeau married Margaret Sinclair in May 1971, in a private ceremony with her family and his brother attending. Their wedding plans had been kept secret from nearly everyone until the last minute. The strain of secrecy had grown a little in Trudeau, who showed tension in the House. At one point he mouthed a curse at a member of the Opposition, but when called out for it claimed that he had merely said "fuddle-duddle."

Margaret was twenty-three years old, and had carefully studied for her conversion to Catholicism before their marriage. She was in many ways a capable young woman who made her own wedding dress, a beautiful and flattering design based on a sari from India. Some newspaper articles referred to her as a flower child, a hippie, and a co-ed. Her parents had emigrated from Scotland and lived in North Vancouver, where her father, James Sinclair, had been elected as a member of Parliament in the Liberal party.

Margaret's Gown

It wasn't long after their marriage Pierre and Margaret Trudeau took a walk one winter night and knocked on the front door of a neighbouring house. They'd noticed the house had a backyard ice rink, and that was enough reason to make friends. The Masons and their children were pleased to make their acquaintance. For many winters, both families formed broomball teams with their friends to play a kind of hockey that would never make it to Hockey Night in Canada.

Trudeau-mania was still running high when the couple had their first son during the first year of their marriage. It was unusual to have a prime minister with a growing family while in office. Before 1971, the last prime minister who became a father while in office was Sir John A. Macdonald.

While it was still the fashion in 1971 for hospitals to keep expectant fathers out of the delivery room, Margaret Trudeau put her foot down. If Ottawa Civic Hospital intended to keep her husband away from her during the birth, she would have the baby at home at 24 Sussex Drive. The hospital's board of directors abolished the ban on fathers in delivery rooms, and in the wake of the Trudeau birth other hospitals began to follow suit in Ottawa and across the country.

While Trudeau's mother Grace was still living at this time, she was badly affected by Parkinson's disease. As well, a form of dementia seemed to limit her communication. She was quiet and friendly with Margaret even if she might not always have understood this was her daughter-in-law. But when her infant grandson Justin was put in her lap, she did understand that this was the child of her son Pierre, and she was delighted. Since she was older and less able, most of the grandparenting of Trudeau's children was done by their mother's parents, the Sinclairs. Jimmy Sinclair particularly enjoyed taking his grandsons fishing.

Three Sons

In all, Pierre and Margaret Trudeau had three sons. Justin was born on Christmas Day, 1971. The second son, Alexandre, was known by the nickname Sacha. His birthday was Christmas Day, 1973. Their third child was Michel, adopted soon after his birth on October 2, 1975.

Michel was of First Nations descent. It is possible to see his adoption as part of a cultural trend from the 1960s to the 1980s which saw thousands of children of Aboriginal descent adopted by Canadians of European descent in an effort to assimilate First Nations or Metis children into what was considered mainstream society. But for Pierre and Margaret Trudeau, there seems to have been no such agenda, only a child who became one of their beloved sons.

Young Justin and Pierre Trudeau

In their home, English was the language usually spoken between Pierre and Margaret, or between Margaret and the children, or with the Sinclair grandparents. French was the language Pierre usually spoke with the children, as his own father had done. Both languages just seemed natural in their household, among the family and the constant stream of household staff and visitors from Parliament Hill.

In years to come as Trudeau travelled in Canada and to other nations, he would take one, two, or all three of the boys with him. At six years old, Justin travelled with his father to Alert Bay at the north end of Baffin Island in Nunavut. While there, one of his father's assistants led the boy through the little town to a workshop, and lifted him up to look through a window. Inside was a man in a red suit, busy at a workbench. Spotting Santa in his workshop near the North Pole was a moment of wonder for the boy, who on other occasions saw his father preparing for meetings with officials in Germany and Russia.

On another occasion, it was Sacha and Michel who accompanied Trudeau on a trip. At one point they waited for their father's attention before saying that their camera wasn't working. Don't worry, Trudeau assured them, you're making memories that will last longer than any photograph.

Each of his sons, as they grew old enough to travel with their father, enjoyed these opportunities for time with their father and the interesting associates and journalists with whom he travelled. Trudeau also would extend his considerate attention to the children of other leaders when they were present at informal or official greetings.

One day, Justin was allowed to meet his father for lunch in the cafeteria near the House of Commons. When he noticed the leader of the opposition sitting at a table across the room, Justin told Trudeau a joke he had heard in the schoolyard. To his surprise, his father rebuked him, saying that one can make fun of a politician's actions, but we do not make personal jokes mocking them as people. Then Trudeau took him across the room to introduce him to Joe Clark having lunch with his own daughter Christina.

Call Signs

In the wake of the October Crisis, the RCMP provided more security for the Trudeau family than had formerly been done for previous prime ministers. In radio transmissions, Pierre was known by the simple code name Maple One. Margaret was Maple Two, and as their sons were born, Justin, Sacha, and Michel were given the code names Maple Three, Maple Four, and Maple Five.

There was no traditional rule book to rely on, so officers working on security duty learned to do what was working best for each kind of situation. It was easiest to provide security when the entire Trudeau family was at home at 24 Sussex Drive, or in the residence at Harrington Lake. But what about when Maple One was working on Parliament Hill, and Maple Two was at home?

Margaret grew annoyed and fretful, feeling she was under constant surveillance. One day she put baby Justin in a stroller and went with him on a fine walk through the neighbourhood by herself. Her security detail lost track of her and were quick to phone Pierre. Most new parents don't need to have unhappy conversations together about ditching security guards.

As time went on, differing attitudes about security became one of several stresses in the Trudeau marriage. It was hard for a man in his fifties and a woman in her twenties to see eye-to-eye on most matters. Margaret was learning her role as a wife at the same time as she was learning to be a mother. As well, she was learning what it was like to be the wife of the Prime Minister of Canada. In many ways the challenges Margaret faced were similar to those later faced by Princess Diana when she married Prince Charles of England in 1981. Even though Margaret had visited Pierre at his official residences while they were dating, she had not realized how much their home and family life would be affected by security concerns and the social interactions necessary for the Prime Minister and his wife.

For his part, Pierre made a serious effort to be home for dinner with his family every evening that he was working in Ottawa. He would also bring two big briefcases of papers to read later that evening, but he'd be home for dinner and a swim in the pool that he'd had installed, one of the few renovations he insisted on at 24 Sussex Drive. Working nine-to-five or six o'clock was a feat of scheduling that can't be matched today by most parents working as lawyers, elected officials, or senior businessmen.

24 Sussex Drive Swimming Pool

In fact, he was usually home as well when the children were eating breakfast, because he needed a full night's sleep. Unlike some leaders of that time who became legendary for keeping long hours, Trudeau had to manage his health with regular hours for rest. He could work on four or five hours' sleep during a crisis, but could not keep this up for years the way Richard Nixon did while president of the United States.

Family Changes

Their sons were still young when Pierre and Margaret decided to separate. The separation was widely reported in the media and lampooned by political cartoonists. The news didn't seem to grow stale as Margaret began dating, as she was seen dancing in clubs with the Rolling Stones. Her struggles with a mood disorder were not overlooked. Though these news stories were uncomfortable for the entire family, the Trudeaus remained in contact. Pierre was now a single father with a more-than-full-time job, but he and Margaret were careful to ensure that she had regular time with their growing sons.

When the boys set themselves the goal of swimming out to a little island in Harrington Lake and back to celebrate turning seven years old, Trudeau was there to swim beside each of them during this personal rite of passage: first Justin, then two years later Sacha, and then Michel.

Each day Trudeau spent with his sons at Harrington Lake, they were likely to spend four hours or more outside, no matter what the weather. Cold or wet weather wasn't a problem if you wore the right clothes, he told his sons. Often they would share a bar of dark chocolate while out in the hills, then go back to the house to warm up and have a meal. Some days he would choose a place on a topographical map of Gatineau Park, and say to his boys "Allons-y," (Let's go there.) By then he was so familiar with the area that he never got lost. If a hiker wandered into the area and across their path, Trudeau would give directions with confidence and aplomb.

When Trudeau left politics in 1984, it was a time of changes for his family. The boys had really come to see the prime minister's residences as their family homes, and they had to adjust to the Art Deco home Trudeau bought in Montreal on Avenue des Pins. As well, by then Pierre and Margaret were divorced. Their boys came to feel a sense of home in their mother's townhouse as well as their father's house with its big windows and walls of art. When Trudeau bought a property in the Laurentian hills just north of Montreal, that became a summer home with a small private lake that reminded them of Harrington. At Trudeau's request, architect Arthur Erickson designed a cabin that could be secured for the winters.

Arthur Erickson

Three Grown Sons

Trudeau's sons were close as children, but did not all follow the same paths as they grew up. All three attended Jean de Brébeuf College, as their father had. When it came time to choose a university, there were distinct differences among the brothers. The elder and middle brothers chose to attend McGill University in Montreal. It was one of the most highly regarded universities in Canada. As well, attending would keep them close to their father and the family home on Avenue des Pins. The youngest brother chose to attend Dalhousie University in Halifax. There he studied microbiology — a science totally separate from their father's academic studies.

During Justin's third year at McGill University, he took a break and drove to Halifax. It was a good chance to spend some time with Michel at Dalhousie. All the brothers had drifted apart to some extent as they began university studies. For Michel, it seemed the campus in Halifax offered him opportunities to get away from the influence of his brothers and his father. For a while, he took time to party hard. During that visit Justin began to understand Michel's need to define his own identity and make his own life.

After his time at Dalhousie, Michel moved to western Canada. "Michel ... carved his own route through life," Justin was later to say of his brother's move to the West, so different from any of the Trudeau men. "He went west for a life in which he wouldn't have to think about the expectations others might have of him."

Though adopted, Michel was a true son of his father. Trudeau had taken his growing boys out into the wilderness many times, and tried to help them have opportunities to find the emotional and spiritual centre that he had found while camping and canoeing and travelling in wild places. This love for the outdoors took root in his youngest son especially, who loved to go skiing and hiking in the Rockies near Rossland, BC. "Michel had built so much of his life around the snow and the air and the mountains and the people around him," was the way Justin described his brother at twenty-three years old. "He was a free spirit, enamoured of the aboriginal culture that flourishes in Canada's most beautiful places, a guy utterly at peace with himself in a way that had so far eluded both Sacha and me."

As adults, all of Trudeau's sons came to terms with the risks faced by those who venture into the rugged backcountry. Justin advocated caution and good planning, and Sacha made his own trips into the North filming documentaries, but Michel skied and snowshoed with intense enthusiasm. Their father had taught him to feel at home taking those risks, calculating the challenges he would meet and the strength he brought to each effort. Michel wasn't yet twenty-two when, while watching a television documentary about Asian burial rites, he said casually, "When it's my turn, just leave me down at the bottom of the mountain where I lie."

CHAPTER 6: BUILDING PARKS

AT THE AGE OF TWENTY-five, Trudeau already knew enough about the effect of wilderness travel on people to write eloquently on the topic. "I know a man whose school could never teach him patriotism, but who acquired that virtue when he felt in his bones the vastness of his land, and the greatness of those who founded it." His essay has been reprinted and quoted many times over the years, in books and articles about Trudeau and the formation of more national parks during his time in office.

In the later years of his life, Trudeau used canoeing as a sustained metaphor when writing in his book titled *Memoirs*:

> *I think a lot of people want to go back to the basics sometimes, to find their bearings. For me a good way to do that is to get into nature by canoe — to take myself as far away as possible from everyday life, from its complications and from the artificial wants created by civilization. Canoeing forces you to make a distinction between your needs and your wants. When you are canoeing, you have to deal with your needs: survival, food, sleep, protection from the weather. These are all things that you tend to take for granted when you are living in so-called civilization, with its constant pressures on you to do this or that for social reasons created by others, or to satisfy artificial wants created by advertising. Canoeing gets you back close to nature, using a method of travel that does not even call for roads or paths. You are following*

nature's roads; you are choosing the road less travelled, as Robert Frost once wrote in another context, and that makes all the difference. You discover a sort of simplifying of your values, a distinction between those artificially created and those that are necessary to your spiritual and human development.

Grassroots Call for Parks

Expanding the system of national parks in Canada was an issue close to Trudeau's heart, but it wasn't one he had to impose on any unwilling region. Banff and Jasper National Parks had been wildly popular, and many citizens were working towards the creation of similar protected zones in their own parts of Canada. The story of one of the resulting parks is a good example of how the expansion of the national park system proceeded in many parts of the country.

Pacific Rim National Park on the west coast of Vancouver Island is a swath of beaches, cliffs, and breathtaking forested slopes. The entire shoreline was very nearly was opened for clear-cut logging, mining, and private ownership of land along the entire coast. But among the few residents of this isolated coast were people who made regular appeals to the federal government and to the province of British Columbia that land should be acquired for an extensive park.

One among these residents was R. Bruce Scott, who in thirty years working at the communication cable in Bamfield had taken a collection of slide photographs of the west coast of Vancouver Island. In the late 1960s Scott showed this collection to every group he could meet in and around Vancouver and the provincial capital of Victoria, particularly to elected officials at any level of government, from local to provincial and federal. His wife ran the projector while Scott spoke of the long beaches between the towns of Tofino and Ucluelet, the Lifesaving Trail along the coast where survivors of shipwrecks could follow the cable line towards rescue, and the islands in Barkley Sound between these shores. Every group signed Scott's petitions to the provincial Parks Branch and the federal Ministry of Recreation and Conservation, asking that these shorelines be acquired and protected as a national park. In May 1967, the petitions were favourably received by the Liberal government of

Canada, but the National Parks Act would have to be changed to allow any newly proposed national park to be created. Only four national parks had been created in the previous thirty-five years, as the federal focus had been on resource development by business instead of preservation of natural environments.

Scott increased his promotion of the park, as did others. The breakthrough came when cabinet minister Jean Chretien attended a fundraising dinner in Victoria. Scott was able to talk Chretien into taking a helicopter flight over the area proposed for Pacific Rim National Park.

Chretien was deeply moved by the experience. A self-described little guy from Shawinigan, he wasn't a white-water canoeist and camper like Trudeau, and it was a new thing for him to see natural places this way. He returned to Ottawa and explained to Trudeau what he had seen that had made him a true believer in the need for more national parks, and for this national park in particular. Trudeau understood what had happened — his friend and colleague had been taken up unto a high place and shown all the wonders of the world, to put it in words from the New Testament. Trudeau trusted the opinions of his friend.

A similar experience at another place came to Trudeau in 1970, when he and a group of friends paddled the Nahanni river in Northwest Territories, through the deepest canyons in Canada. At that time, it was unheard-of for heads of state to go out of reach for days on long river expeditions far from roads. But this trip wasn't an escape from his obligations—it served to remind Trudeau that his mandate was to serve the physical land of Canada as well as its human citizens. As a man who had travelled extensively, he realized that this splendid river was not only a national treasure, but a valuable resource for world history. It would not be enough to declare this river a simple park; the area needed to be protected from resource extraction or over-development.

With Chretien and the Liberal Cabinet ministers, Trudeau changed the National Parks Act to allow the formation of new parks. The National Park System plan, passed in 1970, divided Canada into 39 regions and called for the expansion of the park system so that the characteristic physical, biological, and geographic features of each region would be protected. With this act, the focus of the national park system shifted from recreation to preservation. Nine new national parks were in place by 1972. One of the regions protected was East Coast Boreal Region, where Labrador's Mealy Mountains make up the easternmost part of the Canadian Shield. Another was the creation of Nahanni National Park Preserve. Forillon and La Mauricie were new parks in Quebec, along with Gros Morne in Newfoundland, Kouchibouguak in New Brunswick, and Kluane in Yukon Territory. National parks were no longer entertainment opportunities near cities and major transportation routes. The new parks preserved representative areas of wilderness. Resource extraction by destructive means was no longer the first priority for the regions.

When the premiers met with Trudeau in 1971 to discuss constitutional matters in Victoria, Trudeau took Chretien's advice and made time to tour the area proposed for Pacific Rim National Park. It was everything Chretien had said and more, and everything Trudeau appreciated about wilderness.

The park began as areas between Tofino and Ucluelet, some of the islands in Barkley Sound, and a narrow strip along the Lifesaving Trail, now called the West Coast Trail. Provisions were made to acquire more land along the trail in coming years.

In 1976, Chretien flew over Baffin Island with his wife Aline. Their awe and amazement at that frozen land inspired Chretien to lead in the expansion of new national park Auyuttuq, in the roles in Trudeau's cabinet he held at that time as the Minister of Parks, of Northern Affairs, and also Indian Affairs. That was also the year in which UNESCO (United Nations Educational, Science and Cultural Organization) declared Nahanni National Park a World Heritage Site. By 2015, there were twenty World Heritage Sites in Canada, including both cultural and natural sites. They range from L'Anse-aux-Meadows and Red Bay Basque Whaling Station on the East Coast, Rideau Canal and Waterton Glacier, Head-Smashed-In Buffalo Jump and Dinosaur Provincial Park, to Kluane on the West Coast.

Trudeau was able to visit Pacific Rim and many other national parks, and take a personal enjoyment in the protection of these areas from mining and logging. He brought his family to Pacific Rim and farther north along the coast to the Queen Charlotte Islands which are (now known by their traditional name Haida Gwaii). There the Haida first nations people honoured him as a visiting dignitary, and gave his family traditional dancing blankets as a sign of respect. The blankets were displayed prominently in his home for the rest of his life.

Losing Maple One

During his years in office, Trudeau continued to enjoy day trips canoeing near Ottawa or Montreal, and camping trips on rivers in the Arctic in what is now Nunavut Territory, or Yukon and Northwest Territories. It became almost normal for his friends to invite him for a planned day trip or a last-minute outing, and to see him arrive in a large car or even a stretch limousine with an RCMP officer or two as well as one or more of his sons.

Understandably, the RCMP did not usually train its officers in canoeing skills. On several occasions, Trudeau and his friends would end up rescuing the security detail after the officers' canoe flipped during the first rough water of the day. It took a special kind of patience to be a security officer for Trudeau.

One day, a neighbour phoned Trudeau at the Harrington Lake residence. It was author Bill Mason, maker of the instructional canoe film series *Path of the Paddle*, saying he was taking his children on a day run down the Picanoc River near Kazabazua, Quebec.

Trudeau brought along five-year-old Justin and three-year-old Sacha. Everyone had a marvelous time on the river, in part because that day the RCMP had agreed to see them off as they launched, and meet them down-river at the bridge where they would end the trip.

But there were no RCMP officers waiting when the Trudeaus and Masons arrived at the bridge. No one had a cell phone, of course, in 1977. It began to rain heavily. On that isolated road, there was only one old cottage nearby, so the party trudged up to knock at the door. The French-Canadian couple who answered were slack-jawed with surprise to recognize the Prime Minister at their doorstep, and a wet, muddy troop standing with him. Everyone crowded into the little house with the couple and their friends, and Trudeau borrowed the telephone to call the RCMP. It appeared that the limousine and RCMP truck had been stuck in the mud at the launch site for hours, and were now waiting by the wrong bridge. In no uncertain terms, Trudeau let the RCMP know that Maple One and a very tired Maple Three and Maple Four were to be found right away. While they waited for their ride, the party could only laugh at their predicament. As Bill Mason's daughter later wrote, "Through the paper-thin walls from the other room came the unmistakable sounds of an amorous couple enjoying themselves very thoroughly and intimately."

Trudeau may have been famous for his statement that the state has no place in the bedrooms of the nation, but it appeared the couple felt there was a place for their prime minister *next to* their bedroom. The sound of car tires on gravel outside was a signal for Trudeau to take his party outdoors to meet their ride.

Youth Programs

With Senator Jacques Hébert, Trudeau worked to found and promote two national programs for youth which would promote multicultural understanding. The Canada World Youth program saw young Canadians volunteering overseas. Founded in 1971, by 1973 the CWY program had sent groups of young Canadians to Cameroon, Malaysia, Mexico, Tunisia, and the former Yugoslavia. By 1981, educational programs were run by CWY between Canada and more than 25 countries. Other nations created programs of their own inspired by CWY. By 1997, academic credits were offered to CWY participants. The CWY program is a lasting legacy of Trudeau and Hébert's efforts to encourage Canadian youth to learn what they did from informal travel.

Another youth program founded in 1977 had similar but nationalist goals. Within Canada, the bilingual Katimavik program saw many young citizens volunteer in urban and rural settings across the country. Each Katimavik volunteer was posted to three places for three months each: one urban, one where the language was not the youth's mother tongue, and one in national parks. A lot of benches and trails and campgrounds got established with this volunteer labour. Though honoured by the United Nations in 1985 for environmental involvement, federal funding was interrupted for ten years. It took a hunger strike by Senator Jacques Hébert to renew attention to Katimavik. From 1994 to 2012, the re-structured program expanded successfully. Even when funding was abruptly cancelled under Prime Minister Stephen Harper, Katimavik rallied with help from alumni and community partners. This legacy of Hébert and Trudeau is a particularly versatile program.

Talking The Talk, Walking The Walk

Canada's history and geography wasn't just something Trudeau knew from books, or even from flights to every region of Canada while he was in office. It was something he learned and knew as he walked in the footsteps of explorers and paddled his canoe along routes taken by fur traders. Occasionally, he was able to explore the forests and rivers of other countries, not only during his early backpacking travels, but later in precious days taken between meeting with leaders of other nations. On one of these trips, he paddled parts of Brazil's Rio Negro, a tributary of the Amazon, in a traditional boat.

In 1980 on a flight to a military base in Norway, he was looking attentively out of the helicopter's window down at a rough northern river when he commented to his executive assistant Ted Johnson that he thought the river rapids could be run. He could see the possible track for a canoe to take on river-left. After that, during the four years that Johnson was working for him, canoeing was the conversation subject they preferred when it was possible to relax in transit, take time away from their official duties, and chew the fat, as Trudeau liked to say. "It became a sort of sport for us, on occasional flights over wild country," Johnson said later. "Spot a rapid and figure out an imaginary route through it before it passed out of sight." herever he travelled in the world as a prime minister, Trudeau brought his awareness of what it was like to enjoy wilderness spaces.

CHAPTER 7:
A LONG WALK IN THE SNOW

AS TIME WENT ON, TRUDEAU-mania waned. Not every policy put in place by Trudeau and his cabinet was popular. Their policy on immigration changed the government's focus so that more of the immigrants accepted into Canada were not from Great Britain or western European nations, but from other areas including countries in southeast Asia. This immigration policy change was in direct contrast to Canada's long- standing policies since 1900 which had placed barriers to immigration from India, China, and other Asian countries. The policy of bilingualism in Canada was being expanded to support a multicultural approach for the future. It was surprising to some Canadians how much multiculturalism challenged class privilege, which benefited people of British descent and marginalized people of other ethnic groups.

In 1971, Canada became the first country to adopt multiculturalism as an official policy. Trudeau was working towards his goal of a Just Society, and changes didn't happen overnight. He realised that the essential ingredient of politics is timing — the right decision made at the wrong time can fail.

In 1972, the Liberals returned to power with a minority government, but Trudeau made some bold decisions with confidence. He appointed Muriel McQueen Fergusson as the first woman to be Speaker of the Senate. In cabinet shuffles throughout the rest of his time in government, Trudeau named more women as cabinet ministers than in any previous government.

Boat People

There was a sharp increase in the number of appeals from people who wanted to emigrate from Third World countries to Canada. Between 1971 and 1980, there were over 8,000 Vietnamese immigrants who arrived in Quebec, and more in other parts of Canada. Many of these people were not prosperous business owners who could bring a financial investment to set up their own employment in Canada, as is now preferred for immigrants. These were refugees known as 'boat people' who had escaped in small boats the life-threatening dangers in their homeland. Trudeau and his advisors supported changes to immigration laws which allowed more refugee claims to be accepted. While some of these refugees were educated in French, few spoke any English. Of those who were professionals or skilled labourers, almost none had training recognized by Canadian academic standards.

Trudeau's cabinet announced several new programs to help these immigrants assimilate into English-speaking and French-speaking parts of Canada.

The expense of these new programs were resented by some Canadians who felt it would be better for programs to benefit students and workers who were born here. At one public event a heckler jeered at Trudeau, "Where's your Just Society now?"

"Ask Jesus," Trudeau shot back, over the heads of a crowd. "He brought it up first." His confidence paid off when the Liberals regained a majority government in the 1974 election.

Wage Controls

Inflation was a pressing issue in Canada throughout the 1970s and 1980s, as it was throughout the Western world. Prices were rising faster than wages, and whenever new contracts were negotiated by unions, the wages had to be higher than before in order to meet the workers' needs. The cost of living was higher than it had ever been, and increasing month by month. Canada's wealth of natural resources, though extensive compared to other countries, was not enough to protect Canadians from the global problem of rising prices and wages. The Liberal and Progressive Conservative parties had differing ideas about how to deal with inflation.

Another issue was unemployment. There were more people on Unemployment Insurance than had ever been expected when the program began in 1935 under Prime Minister R.B. Bennett. Usually, in a time of high inflation, there would be a lower rate of unemployed workers; or if there were more workers than jobs, at least prices would not increase at a high rate.

Robert Stanfield, as leader of the Progressive Conservatives, campaigned during the 1974 election on a platform of wage and price controls. Trudeau and the Liberals campaigned opposing the controls he proposed. After winning the election, however, the Liberal policies changed.

In a highly controversial move, Trudeau imposed not only wage controls on contract negotiations for federal civil service jobs, but a national ninety-day freeze on wages and prices in 1975. Not every employed person was affected, but all federal government employees were. The intent was to stop inflation before it reached the runaway pace seen in Germany before the Second World War; to that extent, the wage and price controls put in place by Liberals succeeded. But the freeze was not matched in other countries, and the intersecting economies of the Western nations continued to experience inflation.

The wage and price freeze was not a popular move. It inspired resentment among Conservative party members in particular. High inflation throughout this decade was not contained through wage and price controls.

Trudeau was not popular with separatists in Quebec. Members of the provincial Parti Quebecois resented the federalism of Trudeau, which they saw as the antithesis of their vision for Quebec as an independent sovereign nation. To separatists, Trudeau had sold out the interests of Quebec to *les Anglais*. In 1976, the Parti Quebecois won a provincial election, with René Lévesque as the new premier of Quebec. When Lévesque announced there would be a referendum on whether to separate Quebec from Canada, Trudeau knew he would have to campaign against separation.

Defeating the House

In the spring of 1979, the Liberal Party lost a vote of confidence in the House, and an election was called. Trudeau immediately moved his family out of 24 Sussex Drive into a rented home, and put very nearly all of his furnishings and possessions in storage. He was not able to move down the road to Stornoway, the official residence for the Leader of the Opposition, because it was currently undergoing renovations.

Many people in western Canada felt a growing sense of alienation from the rest of the country. This alienation and economic difficulties were among the factors leading to the defeat of the Liberals in the 1979 election. In 1974 the Liberals held 141 seats in Parliament, with 43% of the popular vote, while the Progressive Conservatives held 95 seats, with about 35% of the popular vote. This time around, the Progressive Conservative party formed a minority government with 136 seats to the Liberals' 114 seats. Joe Clark became the new prime minister, with a caucus of MPs from Ontario and the Western provinces. The Liberals took few seats west of Quebec.

The Liberals' electoral defeat was a blow to Trudeau, who took this moment to resign as party leader for the Liberals. Retiring from politics would be the right thing to do, he felt. His growing sons needed more time with him, and with their mother. Though Pierre and Margaret had separated, and were divorced by 1984, they made it a priority to look after the needs of their children, including time with each of the parents. Margaret took the boys for some weeks right after the 1979 election, so that Pierre could clear his head on a canoeing expedition. He was invited to join seven friends on a trip in the Northwest Territories.

The trip was a great way for Trudeau to assess his life goals. The party canoed from Sifton Lake down the fast- moving Hanbury River. There were a couple of tricky rapids, and rough portages around a waterfall and a canyon, but Trudeau at sixty years old did more than his own share of camp chores and carrying a heavy canoe. When the Hanbury merged with the Thelon River, the group continued on through a game sanctuary to historic sites mapped by explorers and fur traders. As a helicopter flew over their campsite one day, Trudeau joked that it was searching for him because he was wanted in Ottawa as the Conservative government was failing.

Turn Over

The Conservative minority government was shaky from the start, and their comeback to power lasted only nine months. When it became clear that the new budget proposed by Prime Minister Joe Clark would not be popular in the House, Trudeau joined with other Liberals in a last-minute effort to get every Liberal member of Parliament and like-thinking NDP MP to show up for a vote of non-confidence. Not all of the Conservative MPs were able to attend and cast their vote, and the government's proposed budget was defeated. Clark called for an election in early 1980, which he lost.

The Liberal party began to move smoothly back into government offices. One of Trudeau's new assistants was able to persuade him to shave off the ragged beard he had grown over the summer, by saying it reminded her of her new dog. A more important concern was that the House of Commons needed a new Speaker. Trudeau appointed Jeanne Sauvé, the first woman to hold that office, whom he knew as "a fighter" from her six years as a Liberal cabinet minister.

Trudeau's last term in office was devoted to national unity. He acted in support of a national constitution and charter of rights, and in opposition to the separatist goals of the Parti Québécois who governed Quebec. When Lévesque called for Quebec to hold a referendum on sovereignty-association in 1980, Trudeau campaigned vigorously for the "No" supporters.

The National Energy Program

Trudeau's goal of a Just Society had effects on his own efforts to repatriate Canada's constitution, but also on his party's economic policies. The changes that were made to unemployment insurance in particular and many other policy areas complicated the task of the Bank of Canada, which strove to guide the national economy by setting lending rates that would encourage or discourage borrowing of money.

When pressured in 1980 by Alberta businessmen to raise more quickly Canada's price for a barrel of oil to the world price, the prime minister's response was to ask if that was fair. How many people would be penalized if that price were changed too abruptly? Less than a year later in Kenya at a United Nations conference on new and renewable energy sources, Trudeau stated that rising energy costs were an enemy of freedom. The creation of Petro-Canada International was announced, intended to assist developing countries to achieve their own energy self-sufficiency.

Trudeau's methods for managing Canada's energy needs were not appreciated by regions expecting to benefit from the fossil fuel industries. Plans to ensure that Alberta's oil and natural gas reserves would be pipelined to central Canada and the Maritimes were met with resistance. Some oil executives felt that selling the crude oil and processed fuels overseas or to the Americans for immediate profit was a better decision to make.

Many western Canadians resented feeling like eastern Canada was indifferent to the interests of western provinces. "Let the Eastern bastards freeze in the dark," was the opinion expressed in Alberta newspapers by people who had conveniently forgotten that during droughts in the Depression years, cod was shipped from the Maritimes for relief programs in Prairie provinces unable to grow much grain. A recession in the western provinces caused decreased investment in drilling for oil, and the unemployment rate rose. It was easy to blame Trudeau for imposing the National Energy Policy.

At one point in the summer of 1980, Alberta's premier came to meet with Trudeau to consult on energy issues. Peter Lougheed had a different approach to federalism than Trudeau, but they respected one another. It was a warm day when they met at the Harrington Lake residence. To clear their heads, Trudeau suggested that they should take a break to row a boat on the lake. The rowboat was rather dilapidated, and didn't inspire confidence. Lougheed's aide inquired as to what should be done if they did not return. Immediately, Trudeau replied that if they were lost, all of Canada would cheer.

International Relations

While Queen Elizabeth never completely forgave Trudeau for turning a pirouette behind her back after their first meeting, they did get along much better than Trudeau did with Margaret Thatcher. It was no secret Britain's prime minister had differing politics and goals from Trudeau's. They didn't need to exchange harsh words in public for their mutual dislike to be known. At the G7 Summit in 1984, Thatcher bristled when Trudeau and President Francois Mitterand of France would converse in French, even in her presence. She felt deliberately shut out of their discussions.

Justin Trudeau Speaking with Margret Thatcher

THE POLITICS OF US President Ronald Reagan were a similar problem for Trudeau, who tried not to let these differences be an international problem. But the fact was he got along a lot better with an earlier president, Gerald Ford. It was Ford who had insisted that Canada would be a member of the G7 Summit in 1976. Relations between Canada and the United States always have been uneven, as the population and economy of the grew to be many times that of Canada. "Living next to you is in some ways like sleeping with an elephant," Trudeau once joked to a gathering of American press. "No matter how friendly and even-tempered is the beast, if I can call it that, one is affected by every twitch and grunt."

With warmth and his personal charm, Trudeau made friends with many foreign leaders. In 1971 he was touring Asia, with a stopover in India. This was an opportunity for the Canadian Prime Minister to meet with Indira Gandhi, Prime Minister of India. She was ready with other officials when the plane landed, to greet Trudeau and place a garland of marigolds around his neck in a traditional welcome. But during a brief layover in another Indian city, Trudeau had prepared for their meeting. As written by Ivan Head in his biography *Pierre*, he left the plane to meet Indira Gandhi on the airport tarmac, with two garlands held behind his back. When she greeted him, he placed the garlands around her neck to her obvious delight and a roar of approval from the watching crowd.

Constitutional Plans

In his last term in office, Trudeau set out to complete his longer-term goals of repatriating Canada's constitution and drafted a Canadian Charter of Rights and Freedoms. By this point, more than five decades of wrestling with constitutional goals had been done by several parties. The cooperation of the provinces was required to complete this legislation. For this last effort, federal-provincial negotiations took place over eighteen months and were highly contentious, with dissenting ministers and rulings from the Supreme Court and various provincial courts.

"Canada will be a strong country when Canadians of all provinces feel at home in all parts of the country, and when they feel that all Canada belongs to them," Trudeau said in the House and in more than one public speech. "We wish nothing more, but we will accept nothing less. Masters in our own house we must be, but our house is the whole of Canada."

In one last attempt to renew the constitution with the consent of the provinces, Trudeau met behind closed doors in Ottawa with the ten premiers in 1981. Between November 4 and 5, an alliance formed among eight of the premiers during a late-night talk in the kitchen, and was broken the next night as each premier found his resistance could no longer be sustained. There were many positions to accommodate: Quebec's leaders were threatening to declare independence from confederation, there were ambitions for resource extraction and profit in Western Canada, and every province was demanding special powers and considerations. Trudeau was beset on all sides. But he was determined to make Canadians fully independent of Britain, and to entrench a Charter of Rights and Freedoms. The intent was to sever the most important link to Canada's colonial past. Among the clauses of the constitution that needed special effort to ensure agreement were clauses ensuring aboriginal rights and that all the rights mentioned applied to both male and female persons. Individual liberty and minority rights would be guaranteed for the future.

Quebec's Premier René Lévesque was the final holdout who refused to sign the deal. The separatist premier claimed he had been betrayed by his allies in the Gang of Eight, premiers who had allied in the kitchen. During the night of November 5,, after Trudeau went home and Levesque to his hotel room across the river in Quebec the other premiers compromised on their positions. They insisted on a "notwithstanding" clause which would allow provinces to declare certain laws exempt from the charter. The next day, Trudeau and nine premiers signed the deal. A furious Levesque walked out, and spoke of the agreement as the "Night of the Long Knives," precipitating a series of events that came close to breaking Confederation. Consent was finally achieved in 1982, but without the cooperation of Quebec. In a ceremony on Parliament Hill, the Queen and Trudeau signed Canada's new Constitution Act on April 17, 1982.

With his constitutional goal met, Trudeau turned his attention to international affairs, campaigning for world peace and working to improve relationships between industrialized nations and Third World countries. It was during this time that he and Senator Jacques Hébert worked to support the Canada Youth Program and Katimavik.

National Health Care

The national plan for health care in all provinces was first formed under Pearson and passed into law as Trudeau's first formal act as prime minister, but the plan needed changing to equalize payments among the provinces. Twice during Trudeau's time as prime minister, the laws governing national health care were changed for the public administration of a more equal system covering as many treatments as possible. The last of these changes came in December 1983, when it was already clear that Trudeau was planning the last months of his time as prime minister. The Canada Health Act was introduced in Parliament, spearheaded by Monique Bégin, Minister of Health in Trudeau's cabinet. She was proud to know the Canada Health Act was the last Royal Assent signed by Trudeau, with Jeanne Sauvé as the Governor-General he had recently appointed. The resulting medicare program was comprehensive, universal, and portable for people travelling to other provinces for work or studies.

Signing the Canadian Constitution

Even with all the changes brought by the Liberals — or as some Canadians said, because of them — the country still struggled with rising unemployment, a national budget deficit, and inflation, as did most Western nations. The National Energy Program introduced by Trudeau was unpopular. At home, his sons were of an age to benefit from more of his time than before. On a winter night in February 1984, Trudeau took a long walk in the snow, thinking about his reasons for staying in politics. He resolved to retire. At the end of his last day working in the House, his sons came to meet him on Parliament Hill. Together they went to the top of the Peace Tower, climbing the stairs rather than going to the head of the lineup at the elevator. At the top, they looked out over Ottawa together, with Trudeau showing his sons the roof of their home on Sussex Drive, and where to look towards Harrington Lake.

CHAPTER 8: GAINS AND LOSSES FOR AN AGING TRUDEAU

AFTER RETIRING FROM politics in 1984, Trudeau rarely spoke to journalists for newspapers or television. Liberal party member Sheila Finestone took on the seat of Mount Royal, and party representatives still consulted with Trudeau from time to time. Despite his persona as a man still publicly recognized, Trudeau was a very private man. Passers-by would recognize him walking to work at his legal firm or leaving a restaurant, would stop to shake hands and let him go on his way. It happened in Montreal or Toronto, or airports and small towns, and it didn't seem to matter whether the passers-by had ever voted Liberal.

A man who knew how to enjoy modest meals as well as feasts, Trudeau didn't really learn how to cook more than the bare basics of food until after he retired from politics. Lunch at home with his sons was often as simple as tinned soup and celery sticks. Eating with friends was usually done in restaurants, where he would sit with his back to the door. He was careful to pay his own way and to host his friends when possible. He still was notorious for never leaving a good tip. When he was dating Margot Kidder, she often darted back into a restaurant to add ten dollars to the modest tip he'd left on their table. Other women he dated, including Barbra Streisand and Shirley MacLaine, reported similar stories but spoke as well of his personal magnetism and charm.

Pierre Trudeau in His Law Office

In public and at work in his law firm, Trudeau continued to present that appealing persona: well-groomed, wearing simple fine suits with a fresh rose in his lapel.

At home for a quiet evening alone or with old friends, he could relax in an old sweatshirt and cargo pants. When canoeing or camping, he wore the old buckskin jacket or heavy-knit Cowichan sweater he'd had since before his marriage. His gear on canoe trips was as simple as ever: one old pack, an old paddle, and no camera. As always, he preferred making memories to taking photographs.

He travelled the country, campaigning not for the Liberal party but to defend Canada's constitution against the Charlottetown Accord and Meech Lake Accord. He felt it was a mistake for the accords to include a clause which allowed provinces to pass laws contrary to federal legislation, known as the "notwithstanding clause." To him, this clause would undermine the constitution from being consistent across all the country's regions.

A Daughter

While Trudeau's life has been the subject of many books and films, there has been very little has been written of Trudeau's only daughter and youngest child. Sarah Coyne was born May 5, 1991, in a hospital in St John's, Newfoundland. It wasn't until four months after her birth that she came to the attention of news media. It was front page news across the country that her birth certificate listed Trudeau, then aged 71, as her father. Her life has taken place almost entirely outside the public spotlight that was focused on Trudeau's sons during his years as prime minister.

Sarah's mother was Debra Coyne, a 36-year-old lawyer. The relationship between Trudeau and Debra Coyne came about during the constitutional controversies of the 1980s and 90s. Both Coyne and Trudeau were passionate participants, working together to defeat both the Charlottetown Accord and the Meech Lake Accord, and the attempts by Brian Mulroney to re- write the Constitution. There was a short-lived romance between Coyne and Trudeau in the weeks before the Charlottetown Accord was defeated.

Neither Trudeau nor Coyne has said much publicly about their affair; that silence is appropriate from the man who famously said that the state has no place in the bedrooms of the nation. "I don't talk about my private life in public," Deborah Coyne told the *Toronto Star* in 1991. "I just won't comment."

But to the newspapers, anything concerning Trudeau was still grist for the mill. *Maclean's* magazine reported on the 30th anniversary of Trudeau's rise to power, adding the note that he would visit Toronto once a month to see his daughter Sarah. Throughout the 1990s, neighbours in the Brunswick Avenue area would occasionally see Trudeau and his daughter in Jean Sibelius Park. There they would play as the other families did, and he would push Sarah on the swings.

As well, Trudeau is known to have travelled with his daughter at least once. In 1996, he and five-year-old Sarah were in Niagara Falls when they happened to meet Jimmy Carter, a former president of the United States. They lingered there long enough to form a lasting memory for young Sarah of her father in relaxed conversation with a peer and friend.

Hale and Healthy

Well into his senior years, Trudeau remained active and hale. After retirement, he walked daily to work at his legal firm, no matter what the weather. Evenings he would often attend concerts or public events. Often he would travel to visit friends, such as retired diplomat Peter Green in Jamaica; or if he went to Colorado for skiing, he'd visit with Gerald and Betty Ford. While Ford as a former US president always was accompanied on the ski slopes by two secret service men, Trudeau skied without security. It was rare for him to have any security guards after leaving office.

Sacha and one of his friends took a road trip across the USA with Trudeau along for the ride, attempting to travel incognito with a beard and fedora. Whether or not the disguise worked, Trudeau went unrecognized as the trio drove from one fast-food restaurant to the next along their route to an isolated place in the Kentucky hills. The Rainbow Festival was taking place, and Trudeau fit in perfectly, dancing shirtless in the drum circle.

He was active in outdoor sports at an age when many people are retiring into a quiet life at home. While vacationing in the Caribbean in his seventies, he stepped into a hole and ripped his knee. Recovering fully from the surgery, within a few years he was vacationing at Whistler, BC and skiing the black diamond trails as he had for many years before the injury. Frequently, he went on day trips with his friends the Masons, canoeing in the Gatineau. On a 1995 trip down Stikine River in northern British Columbia for an eighteen-day-trip with Ted Johnson and other friends, he ran the rapids with careful analysis from shore, and paddled forty miles every day. Almost any obstacle he faced, Trudeau was able to overcome.

His last journey by canoe was taken on the Petawawa River in his late seventies, paddling in the bow this time but setting a quick pace for the guide looking out for him as stern paddler. He still did more than his own share of camp chores with the guide. He even carried two packs at a time on portages until Ted Johnson warned him that it was bad for the morale of the other men, who were younger by eighteen years and more. On that trip, friends were hovering somewhat nearer to him in their canoes than they used to during previous trips on the Stikine, and on the Hanbury and Thelon rivers.

It was a family joke among his sons that whenever their father went to see a film, he always would insist on paying only the senior citizen's discounted price. Considering Trudeau as a traditional senior citizen was unthinkable. In what were to be the last years of his life, Trudeau continued to work as an author and a law consultant. He struggled with symptoms of Parkinson's disease. Because of this condition, he reduced his attendance of public events, but was not afflicted as badly as his mother had been in her last years. A friend on the board for the Bank of Montreal made sure he had regular invitations to events sponsored by the bank. He was robust and active, until a sudden loss that took his vitality.

The Greatest Loss

PIERRE ELLIOTT TRUDEAU: CHILD OF NATURE

The hardest thing for any parent is the loss of a child, even a grown child. Trudeau had known losses during his adult life. The death of his parents and divorce from Margaret came during his prime, and were blows that he was able to weather with resilience. The death of his son Michel in the autumn of 1998 was a blow from which he was never able to recover.

Kokanee Lake lies at the bottom of a mountain valley near Rossland, BC. It's not a particularly large lake, only about four hundred metres wide, a kilometre long, and very deep. The lake is beautiful, and set among cliffs and steep rocky slopes. To go skiing on the glacier above Kokanee Lake on a bright sunny day was heaven on earth for Michel Trudeau, who had been taught by his father to value breathtaking scenery, the challenge of skiing in a remote wilderness, and the pleasure of finding a rare kind of stillness.

An early-season thaw made sliding snow knock Michel and one of his friends off the steep shoreline and into the deep lake. The friend was able to struggle to shore. Two of their companions were buried in snow and took hours to dig themselves out and go for rescue. If they had been hiking later in the winter, the lake surface would have been frozen hard enough to walk on. They could have hiked safely on the seasonal track down the centre of the lake and watched the small avalanche of snow come down with far less danger.

When the news reached Pierre and Margaret, they reached out to their surviving sons. Alexandre, or Sacha, was in the Arctic filming a documentary in the Arctic. He flew to BC., to represent their family at the recovery effort at Kokanee Lake. After receiving his mother's call in Vancouver where he was teaching, Justin called his father, three time zones ahead, to let him know he was on the way to Montreal. Did he have any more news from the searchers? Trudeau had never been the kind of man who gave himself false hopes. "No," Trudeau said sadly, as Justin later wrote in his own memoir, "and there won't be any news because Michel is gone. The only question now is whether or not they find the body."

Michel's comment about leaving his body at the bottom of the mountain proved prophetic, as divers were unable to find him. There is a sign on the shoreline commemorating the loss of Michel Trudeau at this place on November 13, 1998.

"The lights began to dim in my father's soul when Michel died," Justin was to write later, saying that his father had grown old abruptly. Trudeau did travel a little, attending an event in China to commemorate the Bank of Montreal's presence there since he improved relations between Canada and China. "But from the time we [lost] Michel until his own passing two years later, my father was never the same man."

Passing The Torch

A year before he died, Trudeau came to visit his son Justin where he was teaching in Vancouver. A tour of the school gave a chance for one of the students to run up, asking to speak with Mr Trudeau. This time, it wasn't a star-struck autograph-seeker. It was a student, the daughter of immigrants, saying to her teacher that she'd be late for class that afternoon. To the delight of the father, his son was now "Mr Trudeau" to a new generation of youth.

That winter, Trudeau was in hospital for a few weeks at Christmas with a bout of pneumonia, but recovered with his son Sacha's care and attention. He travelled a little, but not with the energy he used to have for new challenges. Only when the school year was ending in spring did Trudeau permit Sacha to tell Justin that their father had been diagnosed with prostate cancer, and had decided against treatment. This energetic man knew he was now coming to the end of his life.

His sons spent that summer with him, reading to him from his favourite works by Shakespeare, Racine, and Corneille. In the last weeks, they sat quietly with him as he faded. His ex-wife Margaret came to spend time with him as well. His old friend Jacques Hébert, who had been driving and camping around the country to promote Katimavik, cut short the tour to spend one of Trudeau's last afternoons munching chocolate bars and talking about his children, about Katimavik and Canada World Youth, and about the immeasurable beauty of their country. Trudeau died on September 28th, 2000, in Montreal.

At that time, the Sydney Olympics were taking place. In a television interview, Dick Pound, vice-president of the International Olympics Committee spoke of Pierre Trudeau's death, saying in a gentle summation of his friend's life that he hadn't been old long. The Canadian flag was lowered to half-mast in the Olympic athletes' village in Sydney Australia, as it was in Canadian embassies around the world. At home in Canada, flags were lowered in tribute at government buildings, schools, and Royal Canadian Legion buildings across the country.

Before the burial, Trudeau's body was carried by train from Montreal to Ottawa to lie in state on Parliament Hill. Thousands of citizens lined up in a calm procession to pass the casket in the Hall of Honour in the Centre Block. Draped with a Canadian flag, the casket was topped with a quintessentially Trudeau single red rose.

For the return to Montreal, his sons rode with their father's casket, along with some of his old Quebec friends. As the train proceeded slowly through the towns of Ontario and Quebec, the Trudeau sons were deeply moved to see schoolchildren lined up at the stations and along the tracks in tribute. Crowds met the train on arrival in Montreal, and attended the lying in state at the Hotel de Ville. An astonishing variety of mourners filled Notre Dame Basilica for the state funeral. Pallbearers for the service included Trudeau's lifelong friend Roger Rolland, as well as Cuba's leader Fidel Castro and Jimmy Carter, the former president of the USA.

Justin composed a eulogy which he read at the funeral. Knowing that there would be plenty of tributes in newspapers and on television to list the many political accomplishments of Trudeau, his son decided to speak instead of him as a father — an aspect that most people didn't know well. "My friends helped me recall a few stories that anchored the speech," he wrote later in his own memoir. "I put in a few references to the values and vision for Canada that had shaped not just a generation but his own sons, and I tried to offer a little closure to wrap up the outpouring of support from across the country with one last good cry."

In his eulogy, Justin made no mention of his late father's only daughter, Sarah Coyne. Justin's wife, Sophie Grégoire, has since answered media questions with a quiet statement that the two surviving Trudeau brothers have little interaction with their half-sister. During the funeral for Trudeau, nine-year-old Sarah quietly entered the church and accepted condolences from Castro and Carter, then sat in the front row, holding tightly to her mother's arm and to a rose petal. In the years since, while her half-brothers became leader of the Liberal Party and a documentary film-maker, Sarah Coyne has been content to be a student out of the public eye.

"Not many people get to lean on more than 30 million others when their dad passes away," wrote Justin Trudeau afterward in his memoir *Common Ground*. "My dad had a stronger gravitational pull than most, so his absence was bound to leave a deep and lasting void." Both people who admired Trudeau and people who despised him were able to agree that as Canada's most charismatic prime minister, he had a profound and lasting effect upon the country. With the election of his eldest son in 2015, there is once again a Trudeau in the prime minister's office. Memories of the father's policies and actions are being discussed as the son's term begins.

PIERRE ELLIOTT TRUDEAU: CHILD OF NATURE

The Trudeau Tomb

PIERRE ELLIOTT TRUDEAU International Airport

GLOSSARY

24 Sussex Drive: the official residence in Ottawa for the leader of the governing party in the House of Commons.

CBC: The Canadian Broadcasting Corporation, known as Radio Canada in French; the national broadcasting company with both radio and television programming available across the country, including the far North, and world-wide on shortwave radio and on the Internet.

Liberal Party: a national party with roots dating back to Britain's Parliament and the Whigs.

Majority government: when the party with the most seats in the House of Commons has more seats than the other parties put together.

Minority government: when the party with the most seats in the House of Commons is outnumbered by the seats held by other parties.

MP: a member of Parliament.

New Democratic Party: a national party of social democrats which had its origins in Canada's western provinces as the CCF or Canadian Commonwealth Federation, a socialist party.

Parliament: the representatives of Canada's federal government; the House of Commons is filled with members of Parliament who have been elected by Canadians, and the Senate is filled with senators appointed by the prime minister.

Progressive Conservative Party: a national party formed by a union between the Progressives from the Prairie provinces with the Conservative party which had roots dating back to Britain's Parliament and the Tories.

Stornoway: the official residence on Sussex Drive in Ottawa for the leader of the opposition in the House of Commons.

Vote of confidence: when a vote is called on a bill of great importance in the House of Commons, usually on a budget; if the bill is defeated the House is said to have lost confidence in the governing party, and an election is usually called.

TIMELINE

- Birth of Joseph Phillippe Pierre Yves Elliott Trudeau, October 18, 1919
- Jean de Brébeuf College, B.A. 1940
- University of Montreal, LL.L. 1943
- Harvard University, M.A. in Political Economy 1945
- *École des sciences politiques*, Paris 1946-1947
- London School of Economics 1947-1948
- Married to Margaret Sinclair, 1971
- Elected to be 15th Prime Minister of Canada
- First term in office as Prime Minister of Canada, April 20, 1968 - June 4, 1979
- Brief retirement from politics
- Returned to the Liberal Party as party leader, April, 1980
- Second term in office as Prime Minister, March 3, 1980 - June 30, 1984
- Canada's Constitution Act is signed into law by Queen Elizabeth II, April 17, 1982
- Death in Montreal, Quebec, September 28th, 2000

BIBLIOGRAPHY

Bamfield Years: Recollections, by R. Bruce Scott. Victoria, BC: Sono Nis Press, 1986.

Citizen of the World: The Life of Pierre Elliott Trudeau, Volume One: 1919-1968, by John English. Toronto, ON: Knopf Canada, 2006.

Common Ground ,by Justin Trudeau. Toronto, ON: HarperCollins Publishers Ltd, 2014.

Just Watch Me: The Life of Pierre Elliott Trudeau, Volume Two: 1968-2000, by John English. Toronto, ON: Knopf Canada, 2009.

The Last Act: Pierre Trudeau, the Gang of Eight, and the Fight for Canada, by Ron Graham. Toronto, ON: Allen Lane Canada, 2011.

Pierre: Colleagues and Friends Talk about the Trudeau They Knew, edited by Nancy Southam. Toronto, ON: McClelland & Stewart, 2005.

Pierre Elliott Trudeau: The Prankster Who Never Flinched, by Sandra Phinney. Toronto, ON: JackFruit Press, 2006.

Pierre Elliott Trudeau: Why He Paddled, by Jamie Benidickson. Toronto, On: Kanawa, 2001.

Trudeau Revealed by His Actions and Words, by D. Somerville. Richmond Hill, On: BMG Publishing Ltd, 1978.

Trudeau: Images of Canada's Passionate Statesman, edited by Patti Tasko. Toronto, ON: John Wiley & Sons, 2010.

Trudeau's Shadow: The Life and Legacy of Pierre Elliott Trudeau, by James Raffan. Toronto, ON: Random House Canada, 2011.

Trudeau Transformed: The Shaping of a Statesman, 1944-1965, by Max and Monique Nemni. Toronto, ON: McClelland & Stewart, 2011.

The Truth About Trudeau, by Bob Plamondon. Ottawa, ON: Great River Media, 2013.

Young Trudeau: Son of Quebec, Father of Canada, 1919- 1944, by Max and Monique Nemni. Toronto, ON: Douglas Gibson Books, 2006.

Don't miss out!

Visit the website below and you can sign up to receive emails whenever Paula Johanson publishes a new book. There's no charge and no obligation.

https://books2read.com/r/B-A-ZKUK-TWOIB

BOOKS 2 READ

Connecting independent readers to independent writers.

Did you love *Pierre Elliott Trudeau: Child of Nature*? Then you should read *Charles Tupper: Warhorse*[1] by Paula Johanson!

[2]

Not the worst prime minister of Canada, but not by much, Tupper held office for only ten weeks during an election before reluctantly conceding he lost. As a member of Parliament he always kept his doctor's bag under his desk, and Parliament kept two bars open while in session.

There's a famous Canadian painting of the Fathers of Confederation, with John A. Macdonald at the centre of the assembly. But who is the man on the right of the painting, at the focus of their attention? That man in his mutton-chop sideburns is Dr Charles Tupper.

---

1. https://books2read.com/u/brqVWY
2. https://books2read.com/u/brqVWY

Queen Victoria granted him a knighthood for his role in bringing together the Confederation of Canada. He kept Confederation together when his home province of Nova Scotia voted to leave and when Red River voted to join as a new province. Sir Charles Tupper became the sixth prime minister of Canada, but only after his party exhausted all alternatives. At 69 days, his term in office is the shortest yet for any Canadian prime minister. Yet his influence was far greater than that brief term, including policies that were disastrous for First Nations peoples in the Western provinces.

Doublejoy Books is proud to present the second in a series called Prime Ministers of Canada. This series of biographies brings together details of the lives of Canada's prime ministers from Confederation through to the twenty-first century. Look to books in this series for a focus on elements and details that are glossed over in most commentaries on these political figures.

On the book series Prime Ministers of Canada:

To know our Prime Ministers is to take some pride in the eclectic collection of individuals and stories that make up our history. Whatever our politics, whatever one may think of individual PMs and their decisions, one recognizes that they are a mirror to their times, a reflection of who we were and where we come from. Those who do not know our history are doomed to believe it boring; those who do know, gain the bragging rights that come from having great and colourful ancestors.

– Dr. Robert Runté

Read more at books2read.com/paulaj.

Also by Paula Johanson

Alt-Academic
Woolgathering: Awareness of the Foreign in Published Works About Cowichan Woolworking
Sanitizer

Prime Ministers of Canada
Pierre Elliott Trudeau: Child of Nature
Charles Tupper: Warhorse

Slice of Life
No Parent Is An Island
Working Parent
Under The Plow

Young Science
Bat Poop Sparkles
Otters Hold Hands

Standalone

Small Rain and Other Nightmares
Island Views
Plum Tree
Tower in the Crooked Wood
King Kwong: Larry Kwong, the China Clipper Who Broke the NHL Colour Barrier
Science Critters
Green Paddler

Watch for more at books2read.com/paulaj.

About the Author

Paula Johanson is a Canadian writer. A graduate of the University of Victoria with an MA in Canadian literature, she has worked as a security guard, a short order cook, a teacher, newspaper writer, and more. As well as editing books and teaching materials, she has run an organic-method small farm with her spouse, raised gifted twins, and cleaned university dormitories. In addition to novels and stories, she is the author of forty-two books written for educational publishers, among them *The Paleolithic Revolution* and *Women Writers* from the series *Defying Convention: Women Who Changed The World*. Johanson is an active member of SF Canada, the national association of science fiction and fantasy authors.

Read more at books2read.com/paulaj.

About the Publisher

Doublejoy Books is the publisher of a variety of eclectic books of Canadian literature.
   http://doublejoybooks.com
   http://books2read.com/paulaj

www.ingramcontent.com/pod-product-compliance
Lightning Source LLC
Chambersburg PA
CBHW031653040426
42453CB00006B/297